works by amanda lovelace

the
women are some kind of magic
poetry series:

the princess saves herself in this one (#1)
the witch doesn't burn in this one (#2)
the mermaid's voice returns in this one (#3)

slay those dragons: a journal for writing your own story

believe in your own magic: a 45-card oracle deck & guidebook

---

the
things that h(a)unt
poetry duology:

to make monsters out of girls (#1)
to drink coffee with a ghost (#2)

---

the
you are your own fairy tale
poetry trilogy:

break your glass slippers (#1)
shine your icy crown (#2)
unlock your storybook heart (#3)

---

flower crowns & fearsome things
(a stand-alone poetry collection)

---

cozy witch tarot: a 78-card tarot deck & guidebook

---

your magical journal: a place for self-reflection, spellwork,
and making your own magic

make your own magic

a beginner's guide to self-empowering witchcraft

amanda lovelace

illustrated by raquel aparicio

RUNNING PRESS
PHILADELPHIA

Running Press
Hachette Book Group
1290 Avenue of the Americas, New York, NY 10104
www.runningpress.com
@Running_Press

First Edition: March 2024

Published by Running Press, an imprint of Hachette Book Group, Inc.
The Running Press name and logo are trademarks of Hachette Book Group, Inc.

The Hachette Speakers Bureau provides a wide range of authors for speaking events. To find out more, go to www.hachettespeakersbureau.com or email HachetteSpeakers@hbgusa.com.

Running Press books may be purchased in bulk for business, educational, or promotional use. For more information, please contact your local bookseller or the Hachette Book Group Special Markets Department at Special.Markets@hbgusa.com.

The publisher is not responsible for websites (or their content)
that are not owned by the publisher.

Print book cover and interior design by Susan Van Horn.

Library of Congress Cataloging-in-Publication Data has been applied for
ISBNs: 978-0-7624-8414-0 (hardcover), 978-0-7624-8416-4 (ebook)

Printed in the United States of America

LSC-C

Printing 1, 2023

to the sad young girl who
once thought herself magicless:

oh, my sweet autumn child,

you were wrong
in the most beautiful way.

contents

a note from the author

hello there, reader!

welcome to *make your own magic: a beginner's guide to self-empowering witchcraft*.

if you had told me when i was fifteen that i would one day be writing a book like the one you now hold in your hands, i doubt i would have believed you. in fact, i probably would have laughed in your face.

except for the fact that i didn't laugh very much at all those days.

truth is, i was a deeply, deeply unhappy person for much of my life. the traumatic experiences i had at an early age made me see the world as a hopeless and unpleasant place. in my eyes, this wasn't a place where something like magic was even *close* to possible.

oh, sure, maybe in the pages of the fairy tales and fantasy worlds i escaped into every chance i had, but not here.

never here.

i had always been inexplicably drawn to witchy things, but most of the witchcraft books i picked up as a teen were intimidating as *hex*. they made magic seem extremely complicated, using a bunch of words and terms i didn't understand and requiring ingredients someone like me just didn't have access to.

back then, my long-held dream of being a witch seemed way too unrealistic, so i turned my focus away from it for a while, thinking it was a waste of my time and energy.

it wasn't until i came across easy-to-digest, short-form online content in my early twenties that i finally felt brave enough to cast my very first spell. i started by taking something i was already doing every day—making and drinking coffee—and found a way to make it magical. (yes, i'll teach you!) for a long time, that was all i was brave enough for, but even that was enough to add some sparkle back into my eyes.

fast-forward to now, and most of my days are filled with magic, both big and small.

(but mostly just small.)

while big, complicated spells can be fun, they certainly aren't required for someone to be a witch. small and simple magic that doesn't stress you out is valid. small and simple magic that doesn't drain your bank account is valid. small and simple magic that makes your day-to-day just a little bit brighter is valid.

luckily, much has changed since i was a young and aspiring witch. we now live in a world where witchcraft is trending across every social media platform and where they sell beginner-friendly witchcraft books at most major department stores. this book, however, is the one i wish i had had when i was an overwhelmed beginner, when i so desperately wanted a more experienced hand to hold while i figured it all out.

i never want anyone to feel as lost as i did, so you won't find anything too fancy or elaborate here—just a safe and understanding place where you can start building the witchcraft practice that's right for you.

by the time you reach the last page, i hope you will have allowed yourself the joy of making a little magic of your own.

laced with love,
amanda

to the brim she was filled with
moonbeams & starlight,
which she consciously kept dim.

in her mind, it made sense,
for it was a lot easier to pretend
that she wasn't capable
of shining so much brighter.

if i could, i would go back & tell her,
"no one ever said making magic
was going to be easy."

—*living up to your fullest potential rarely ever is.*

part i

the basics

"so, what makes a witch?"

pop culture is absolutely filled with fictional witches, so when you hear someone say the word *witch*, your mind might immediately go to the halliwell sisters from *charmed* (both the original and the reboot), or bonnie bennett from *the vampire diaries*, or perhaps even sabrina from *sabrina the teenage witch* (or *chilling adventures of sabrina*).

they're all amazing characters who have undoubtedly touched many people (especially those of us in the queer community, who often see ourselves reflected in these magical outcasts), and their creators may have even been inspired by real witches, but they don't quite represent what witches in our world are actually like.

more often than not, actual witchcraft looks a lot less like summoning literal hellfire and a lot more like summoning a little self-confidence.

though every witch ultimately practices differently (wouldn't it be boring if all of us were the same?), for many, including myself, being a witch is about recognizing that we have the magic within to bring just about anything we want into existence. we don't just sit around and wait for life to happen to us—we step up and take matters into our own hands.

where we once felt power*less*, we now feel power*ful*.

"can i be a witch?"

short answer: yes.

slightly longer answer: absolutely. everyone has the potential to make their own magic. whether or not you *choose* to call yourself a witch is entirely up to you.

"how do i make magic?"

most of the time, witches make their magic by casting something called—you probably guessed it—a spell!

you've almost certainly done something spell-like at least once before.

you know when you close your eyes and make a wish as you blow out your birthday candles every year? that's very similar to a manifestation ritual.

the difference is, when a witch casts a spell, they don't usually make a wish.

in my practice, i like to claim the thing i want as mine and trust that it will happen, because my will alone is powerful af.

my spells usually start off with an intention in the form of a self-empowering affirmation. it's pretty painless to create one; all you have to do is take the thing you want to happen (e.g., something external like growing a beautiful spring garden or something more internal like having complete and total trust in the path you're on) or the thing you want to become (e.g., confident, inspired, or peaceful), and say it as though it's already true. that means you have to say it in the present tense.

as a witch, you wouldn't ask, "can i *pretty please* remain strong through this difficult situation?"

no—you would firmly declare, "i am a strong badass that can handle anything life throws at me, including this."

see the difference?

while words can certainly be effective by themselves, for a witch, what makes them even more so is combining them with things like actions and tools. the more energy and focus you put into your spell, the more powerful—the more *real*—it will become.

spells can be onetime things, but if you keep repeating that spell (or similar variations of it), then it becomes something called a *ritual*. (this is true of so many mundane daily activities, too. do you drink coffee every morning or herbal tea every night? those are rituals!) rituals also tend to be a little more involved than your everyday spells, especially because they can be perfected and built upon over time.

on witches, pagans & wiccans

there's often some confusion around the difference between being a witch, being a pagan, and being a wiccan, which is understandable, so i thought i would clear it up a little!

◆ a witch—someone who practices witchcraft, which often includes casting spells, taking part in rituals, and working in tune with nature. witchcraft isn't necessarily religious. people of any religion (or lack thereof) can be witches.

◆ a pagan—someone who practices a pagan religion. *pagan* is an umbrella term that encompasses many nature-based religions. to oversimplify, pagans often honor more than one god and/or goddess (this is called *polytheism*) and many—but not all—pagans practice witchcraft and consider themselves witches.

◆ a wiccan—someone who follows the wicca religion, a branch of paganism founded in the mid-1900s. wiccans often (but not always) believe in a dual god and goddess and live by a set of principles called "the wiccan rede." though many wiccans practice witchcraft and call themselves witches, not all do.

because of the popularity of wicca in the late twentieth and early twenty-first centuries, wiccan beliefs and traditions have influenced how many witches practice modern witchcraft today, even if they don't realize it. though *make your own magic* is a book about witchcraft as i see it, not paganism or wicca, you will definitely see some pagan and wiccan influences, such as the wheel of the year (more on this later).

still confused?

◆ like all catholics are christian, **all wiccans are pagan.**

◆ like not all christians are catholic, **not all pagans are wiccan.**

◆ though it often *is* the case, **not all pagans and wiccans are witches** or practice magic.

◆ **anyone can be a witch**—not just pagans or wiccans—regardless of their religion.

your magical journal

next, it's important that you start a magical journal. (you may hear some witches refer to this as a *grimoire* or a *book of shadows*, but i'll be referring to it as a *magical journal*.)

honestly, any old composition notebook you have lying around will do, but i recommend getting a big binder if possible so you can easily add things and move them around. if you prefer a little more direction from your magical journal, you can also look for a guided one where another witch has offered prompts to start you off—i have put one of these together myself!

of course, it *is* the twenty-first century, and most of us are at least a little tech savvy, so you may instead choose to keep a "magical journal" file going on a reliable computer, phone, or tablet. (no matter what anyone else says, a magical journal is *not* less magical just because it's electronic.)

your magical journal is a place where you can reflect upon where you are in your witchcraft journey as well as your life, take note of all the things you've learned (from this book and from others, as well as from any other sources you stumble upon, such as videos or information from witchy peers), and record details about things like spells, rituals, and tarot/oracle card readings.

you'll notice that from this point on i include magical journal prompts on some pages. these are intended to help you get the ball rolling on the self-reflection front. i hope that they'll inspire you to discover magic in every area of your life.

having all of this information at your fingertips will make you a stronger witch over time—trust me. i, for whatever reason, decided not to keep a magical journal for the first few years of my practice, and i regret that decision every day. there's so much progress i can't look back on, and there's nothing i can do to change that.

be better than i was.

if my experience is anything to go by, you'll likely have many magical journals over the course of your practice, so try not to put too much pressure on yourself to make your first one perfect. the way your craft *looks* isn't nearly as important as the way it makes you *feel*. though it may be tempting, it's not necessary to go out and buy a hundred dollars' worth of stickers and pens to make it pretty. be as realistic as possible and remember that you can still make it authentically *you* on a budget.

MAGICAL JOURNAL PROMPT: *think about the magical journey that lies ahead. what are you most excited about? what are you most afraid of? let it all out. mark this entry and make sure to come back to it at some point in the future so you can see just how far you've come.*

your magical altar

now that you have your magical journal, it's time to find a place for your very first magical altar—a dedicated space where you can work your inner magic in the form of spells, rituals, divination, meditation, and more.

it can be anywhere: a bookshelf, a bedside table, a tray. it doesn't have to be anything too extravagant; just make sure it's clean and you have enough room to do your magic. (keep in mind that you can always switch altar spaces later if you need to! you're not beholden to the first space you choose if you outgrow it or it's just not working for you anymore.)

another thing to keep in mind is your personal comfort level. if you live in a house with other people, ask yourself if you think they would be open-minded about you practicing witchcraft. if you're 100% certain that they would be, then you might consider setting up a permanent altar out in the open. but if you live with close-minded or unsafe people, you might want to choose something like a container or box you can hide and take out when you have privacy.

however, i think you'd be surprised how many times people have seen my altar and had no idea what they were looking at. after all, just about everybody has things like crystals and candles in their homes these days!

not being accepted

thanks to its popularity on social media platforms such as tiktok and instagram, witchcraft is becoming not only more and more popular but more and more *understood*.

sadly, despite that, some still refuse to open their hearts and minds to it.

be warned that there are plenty of people out there who continue to believe the misconceptions that witchcraft is evil and that witches only ever have ill intent, even though that couldn't be further from the truth. they may even use harmful religious rhetoric to try to convince you that you're a bad person who's doing bad things.

please know that you don't deserve any of it.

don't *ever* be afraid to be your true self, no matter what anyone else says.

it may break your heart when the people you love don't accept you; the good news is that there *will* be tons of people who not only understand you but practice witchcraft, too. if you're not sure how to find witches in your area, just go to your local witchcraft store and ask about events and gatherings. if all else fails, scour the corners of the internet (e.g., facebook or discord) for some supportive online groups to join!

MAGICAL JOURNAL PROMPT: *do you plan to tell people that you're a witch, if that's how you choose to identify? if so, how will you explain it to them? it's always good to have some talking points prepared, especially if you're nervous about how they'll react. if you choose not to identify as a witch, how will you explain your magical practice if asked about it?*

some people refer to concealing their witchy side from others for fear of judgment as *being in the broom closet*. i can't remember if i've ever used this term in the past—for a long time, i never thought too deeply about its meaning—but i've decided i definitely won't going forward. this phrase is clearly a spin on the idea of being in the closet as a queer person, and speaking from my experiences with both, the two can't be equated and i don't think it's appropriate to do so, though that's just one witch's opinion. feel free to write about your thoughts about this in your magical journal!

don't you dare
paint over your moth wings

just because someone
told you they prefer butterfly wings.

—*yourself is the most beautiful thing you can be.*

your magical altar feat. you

your inner magic is what makes all other magic possible, so it's only right that you place something on your altar to recognize and honor this part of yourself.

first, let me ask you this: *when you think of all the amazing things that you're capable of, what is it that you see?*

perhaps it's an art piece you created.

perhaps it's an award or a trophy for one of your achievements.

perhaps it's a polaroid of yourself during one of your happiest moments, like a birthday or graduation.

don't overthink this part too much!

the symbol of your inner magic can really be anything, so long as it's significant to you. just go with the first thing you think of.

whatever you decide on, go ahead and place it front and center on your altar because it's now going to be the focal point—*you* are going to be the focus, the center of it all.

feel free to add things over time, or even switch them out periodically. i usually place the most recent book i've written or deck i've cocreated, replacing it once another has been published. my writing is part of my magic.

MAGICAL JOURNAL PROMPT: *if you're stuck, ask yourself,* **what's something that makes me proud to be me?** *and freewrite (putting pen to page and writing continuously with no filter) for five minutes until you come up with something.*

your magical tools

magical tools give you a way to direct your inner magic. they help you bring it physically and energetically to life.

a good portion of your altar should be practical and suit your personal magical needs. on the next few pages are some basic tools you might want to consider stashing on, in, or around your altar. (it's helpful to have some drawers, shelves, and/or boxes nearby for this purpose.)

i know, i know, it seems like a lot, but try not to get too overwhelmed by this list.

these are all things you can obtain gradually over the span of your practice. if you need something and don't have the means to obtain it, then be a resourceful witch and substitute it with something you already have on hand.

for example, if you don't have a jar, that's fine, just clean and use an empty jam jar instead. if you don't have a clear quartz crystal, that's fine, too, just find and use a nice rock—those work the same and are (usually) free. make your practice suit *you*, not the other way around.

"welp, that should be good enough!" is basically my favorite phrase as a witch.

◆ your magical journal

◆ a writing utensil

◆ sheets of scrap paper—these will have endless uses, including writing down affirmations.

◆ a white candle—considered by many to be the all-purpose candle because the color white contains every color. (can't have an open flame in your home? opt for a battery-operated candle instead!)

◆ a lighter or matches—used to light candles. also used to burn paper or herbs.

◆ a candlesnuffer—to safely put out your candles.

◆ a candlewick trimmer—to trim your candlewicks before each and every use. (untrimmed wick = large flame = danger!)

> **whenever fire is involved in spellwork, make sure you use caution and follow fire safety!**

◆ dried rosemary—considered by many to be the all-purpose herb due to its myriad properties. (good to have in its plucked leaf form and dried bundle form, as the latter can be used for smoke cleansing.)

◆ a clear quartz crystal—considered by many to be the all-purpose crystal, as it can amplify any intention you give it.

◆ dried roses—considered by many to be the all-purpose flower for the same reason rosemary is for herbs—so. many. magical. properties! (plus, they're very easy to find.)

◆ divination tools such as a tarot deck, an oracle deck, and/or a pendulum—for self-reflection and guidance, among other uses.

◆ a cauldron or firesafe dish—for burning paper and herbs in, or for putting water in.

◆ a bell—a great cleansing and protection tool.

◆ jars, cups, and bowls of all shapes and sizes—i can't even emphasize how many uses these have. for starters, you can store herbs and ingredients in them, and many spells are even contained within them.

◆ drawstring pouches—like jars, cups, and bowls, you can store herbs and ingredients in them and many spells are even contained in them— these are known as spell bags.

all-purpose tools

you probably noticed that i suggested a few all-purpose tools: a white candle to replace any candle, dried rosemary to replace any herb, a clear quartz crystal to replace any crystal, and dried roses to replace any flower.

you should be aware that there's been a lot of debate among witches whether or not all-purpose tools should be encouraged, because, according to some, there are more specific and effective tools a witch could instead use.

personally, i believe that the intention a witch has when using their tools as well as their own personal correspondences are what truly matters when it comes down to it. i also think that anything that makes someone's witchcraft journey just a little bit easier—especially at the beginning— should be seen as a positive thing.

you can consider these all-purpose tools a mere starting point, or a way to substitute whenever necessary.

it's up to you.

"personal correspondences?"

yep!

most magical tools have established magical correspondences that you can find in books or by doing an internet search. while i see the importance of them, i think a witch's personal correspondences are *way* more important.

even if you don't think you do, you have thoughts and experiences that give you a unique perspective on the world, and that unique perspective is going to make your spells even more special and powerful, because your magic is ultimately tailored to *you*.

next you'll find lists of established correspondences for tools like candles, herbs, and crystals that you can use as a reference when doing spellwork, but whatever you do, don't consider them your holy grail.

say that, for example, a happiness spell calls for a yellow candle because that's the established correspondence. cool. but maybe when *you* think of happiness, you think of blue because of a memory you have of a fun day spent swimming in the ocean. or maybe the color blue just makes you super-happy and you can't explain it. use that instead!

your candles

- ◆ white (all-purpose candle)—cleansing, peace, and protection

- ◆ black—antinegativity, banishment, and protection

- ◆ gray—balance, calm, and rest

- ◆ red—confidence, self-empowerment, and strength

- ◆ pink—compassion, nurturing, and self-love

- ◆ orange—ambition, creativity, and justice

- ◆ yellow—intelligence, joy, and positivity

- ◆ green—growth, prosperity, and self-worth

- blue—healing, inspiration, and truth

- purple—intuition, magic, and wisdom

- brown—grounding, security, and stability

- gold—luck, power, and success

- silver—dreams, meditation, and self-reflection

candles, as you probably know, come in various shapes and sizes. some of the most popular among witches are tealight and chime candles, as they're smaller and tend to burn relatively quickly compared to larger types; however, you may use candles of any size, and you may find that you develop your own preference over time. scented candles are fine, too, but it's even better when you use a scent that's associated with your spell's purpose.

one of the simplest spells you can do is to light a candle while saying an affirmation. for example, if you need a quick dose of self-love, you could light a pink candle and say something like, "i am as kind to myself as i am to other people." if you have time, let the candle burn all the way down; if not, go ahead and extinguish it (no, this won't mess anything up) and relight it whenever you have a chance.

your flowers & herbs

- ◆ bay leaves—banishment, manifestation, and money magic

- ◆ chamomile—positivity, prosperity, and soothing

- ◆ cinnamon—energy, self-empowerment, and warmth

- ◆ lavender—calm, intuition, and rest

- ◆ peppermint—abundance, healing, and luck

- ◆ rose (all-purpose flower)—beauty, love, and self-love

- ◆ rosemary (all-purpose herb)—cleansing, protection, and remembrance salt is always great to have on hand. both table salt and sea salt can be used for any cleansing and protection. pink himalayan salt is great for gentle cleansing, especially in self-love spells. black salt is great at helping keep negativity at bay.

edible herbs and flowers can be added to your recipes or ready-to-eat food. (always do your due diligence to make sure the ones you're using are safe to eat.) not only do they add flavor to your meal, but they also add their magical properties. for example, if you require a little boldness, sprinkle some cinnamon onto your toast or oatmeal while saying, "i am fearless in the pursuit of my goals today." yup, it's really that easy!

your crystals

◆ amethyst—calm, intuition, and wisdom

> most amethyst you'll be able to find comes in shades of purple, but my personal favorite is pink amethyst. i find that it inspires just enough self-love for me to be able to trust my intuition without hesitation. if you can get your hands on one, you might find it helpful if you have trouble trusting your intuition as well.

◆ aquamarine—self-expression, tranquility, and truth

◆ black tourmaline—antinegativity, antiworry, and protection

◆ citrine—ambition, joy, and manifestation

- clear quartz (all-purpose crystal)—clarity, cleansing, and healing

- moss agate—abundance, grounding, and growth

- rainbow fluorite—creativity, focus, and individuality

- rainbow moonstone (also called *white labradorite*)—harmony, self-reflection, and new beginnings

- rose quartz—beauty, gentleness, and self-love

- tiger's-eye—confidence, courage, and self-empowerment

when buying crystals, look for shops that source theirs ethically. if you're not sure, ask the shop directly. gather that information and do your own research. do they harm the earth with their crystal mining methods? are their workers treated fairly? these are both important things to consider.

the simple act of carrying a crystal can be a spell. first, pick one with energy you'd like to match and cleanse it (see pages 23–24). next, charge it with your intention by holding it and saying an affirmation. for example, you might pick black tourmaline and say, "my worries do not rule me, nor do they hold me back from having positive life experiences." after, put it in your pocket or in a bag. some witches make jokes about sticking crystals in their bra. while hilarious (and convenient), i wouldn't advise that since it can become a sweaty place and some crystals are susceptible to water damage!

disappearing crystals

as you work more with crystals, you may notice that some will disappear.

for example, some years ago, i bought a beautiful twin clear quartz necklace from a small pop-up crystal shop in the mall. the woman who sold it to me said that twin clear quartz crystals can attract your soulmate.

sadly, i ended up misplacing the necklace only a few months after wearing it nonstop. it was just . . . gone. without a single trace. i searched my house high and low for years on end, never once coming across it. i *loved* this necklace, so i still think about it from time to time.

though disappearing crystals may be frustrating, they can actually be a *good* thing.

i didn't have the perspective back then, but it makes total sense that my twin clear quartz necklace disappeared when it did.

the truth is, i never really needed it in the first place, because i had already met my now-spouse at that point. i'm still undecided about whether or not i believe in soulmates, but if they are real, then my spouse is definitely mine.

i think some crystals find you when you need them the most and depart once you don't need them anymore. *where* they go and *how* they go, i'm not so sure. you can decide for yourself what you want to believe. some say it's faeries (a topic for a much different book), but who knows? i like to think they go to someone who needs their magic much more than you do.

> your crystals might break from time to time, too. if it's in an unusual or unexpected manner, that could also mean your crystal is done serving its purpose in your life. regardless, if this happens, you can give it back to mother earth by burying it somewhere outside or even in the soil of a potted houseplant.

cleansing your crystals

everything has its own unique energy, including our magical tools. that's why we use them, after all—to complement and boost our spell's purpose!

however, they can also *pick up* extra energy from the people, places, and things nearby, and this energy isn't always going to be the most uplifting or positive—it can sometimes be heavy or negative, or simply not vibe quite right with yours.

not only that, but if they sit around for too long, their energy can become stale.

crystals, in my experience, have a particular knack for this kind of energy-shifting.

that's why i think it's so important that you magically cleanse them before using them in spellwork. (make it a habit to regularly cleanse *all* of your tools—minus the ones with cleansing properties already—and your altar space, too.) that negative, unwanted, or stale energy has the potential to mess with the results of your spellwork, and nobody wants that.

here are some ways you can cleanse your crystals:

moonlight cleansing—can be done under the cleansing light of the full moon. you don't necessarily have to put your crystals outside; just leave them in a window that gets a lot of moonlight and move them in the morning. (some crystals can fade or become damaged by sunlight, so make sure you move them out of harm's way asap when you wake up.)

smoke cleansing—can be done with incense or a dried herb bundle of your choice. using a lighter or match, ignite your bundle, wait for the flame to go down and turn to smoke, and then wave the smoky bundle in the space around your crystal until all feels well.

one of the most controversial topics in the witchcraft community today surrounds the use of white sage. not only is it being over-harvested, but it's also an important and sacred herb used by several Native American cultures, such as the Lakota Nation, making this situation all the more dire. i encourage you to opt for a more ethical alternative, whether it's another type of sage—of which there are hundreds—or my favorite, rosemary.

sound cleansing—can be done with an instrument such as a bell. not only are they easy to use at a moment's notice, but they're good for witches (like me) who are sensitive to smoke. simply take your bell in hand and ring it around the crystal a few times. this will vibrate away any icky energy.

cleansing yourself

speaking of cleansing—it's time to learn how to cleanse your *own* energy.

not only can these cleansing methods uplift you in general, but they can help you prepare before spellwork by removing any negative, unwanted, or stale energy attached to you that doesn't match the magic you're trying to create.

here are a few ways you can do so:

dance—put on some taylor swift—or another artist of your choice—and get right to it. while you dance your heart away, your movements will shake off any "blah" energy. if possible, try to do this for the length of one entire song.

shower—you have to shower to get physically clean, so why not make it an energetic cleanse, too? as you wash away the soap, imagine the energy you don't want on you going right down the drain, never to be seen again.

use smoke—yep, you can smoke cleanse yourself, too! just break out your rosemary bundle, light it, and (safely) wave the smoky wand in the space surrounding your body.

> your phone can collect all kinds of negative energy (especially since social media can be such a toxic thing), and if it's always near you, like it is for so many of us, it can put you in a bad mood. for this reason, i highly recommend cleansing your phone regularly. you can do this by ringing a bell around it like you would a crystal, or you can open up a playlist on your phone and put on a feel-good song— just leave it facedown somewhere and let those happy vibrations take care of it!

MAGICAL JOURNAL PROMPT: *start by cleansing your phone every day for at least a week. when the week is up, come back to your magical journal. what differences did you notice, if any at all?*

mother earth

witches have a long-standing reputation of loving, respecting, and working with mother earth.

not only does she provide us with life-sustaining resources such as food and water, but she also blesses us with heart-stopping beauty like forests and oceans. on top of that, she's super-magical, too. after all, where do you think we get the tools that help us with our spells—the herbs, the crystals?

that's right: from our ever-lovely and ever-generous mother earth.

she also made our very existence possible, and therefore our inner magic. it's no wonder so many witches try to do their part to take care of her and keep her thriving, especially in a time when she's at her most vulnerable due to our current climate emergency.

here are a few ways *you* can do your part:

◆ go low- or no-waste

◆ eat locally, vegetarian, or vegan

◆ go thrifting instead of buying new stuff

◆ sign earth-friendly petitions

◆ donate time or money to environmental groups, or take part in a climate event (e.g., a nature cleanup)

◆ vote for political candidates who promise to take on climate change

with those suggestions in mind, focus on what *you* can do. try not to feel guilty if certain things aren't feasible for you for whatever reason; you are not a bad witch, i promise. in a perfect world, we would all have the same time and resources available to us, but we don't live in a perfect world. far from it.

MAGICAL JOURNAL PROMPT: *write about one to three things you can realistically do to be more environmentally conscious in your daily life. how do you plan to hold yourself accountable?*

there is nothing that
feels more holy or
life-affirming to her
than the smell of
the soil after it rains.

—*petrichor.*

the pentacle

i wouldn't be surprised if you've been told that the pentacle—a five-pointed star enclosed in a circle—is a symbol of evil, as this is a very common misconception. in reality, pentacles are a symbol of mother earth. each of the five points on the star represents one of her elements, and the circle surrounding it connects them all as one. for many witches, it's a sacred and protective symbol.

each element has its own correspondences, including:

- earth—north | green | stability, nature, and prosperity

- fire—south | red | passion, creativity, and energy

- air—east | yellow | intellect, ideas, and communication

- water—west | blue | cleansing, emotion/intuition, and inspiration

> just to be clear, *mother earth* encompasses the entire planet as well as her energy, whereas *earth* is just one of her elements.

you'll notice that the pentacle has a fifth element that you may not have learned about before: spirit. spirit can represent many things, but for the sake of this book, it represents you, the witch—your essence, your soul, your inner magic, working in complete and total harmony with the four other elements.

mother earth on your magical altar

you've already placed something on your altar to represent spirit—*you*.

many witches, including myself, also choose to represent mother earth's four main elements on their altar as a way to honor our connection to one another, as well as to invite her magical energy into our spellwork.

want to represent mother earth on your altar? below are a few suggestions for things you can place there (and yes, use in your magic!). it's not required, but you can choose your items based on the element's corresponding color or place them in its corresponding cardinal direction.

- earth—a crystal/stone, a jar of herbs/flowers, or deer/elf imagery

- fire—a cauldron, a candle, or fox/phoenix imagery

some witches place a cauldron on their altar to represent the element of water, as it's a vessel that can be filled with it. personally, i only ever burn things in mine, so i associate it more so with fire. consider both perspectives and come to your own conclusion!

◆ air—a bell, incense/a smoke bundle, or hummingbird/faerie imagery

◆ water—a cup or mug, a seashell, or dolphin/mermaid imagery

MAGICAL JOURNAL PROMPT: *to connect with mother earth is, in many ways, to connect with yourself. you may not even realize how much you reflect the elements, both physically and metaphorically. take out your magical journal and explore some of the ways the four main elements may show up in your life:*

◇ *your inner earth—describe a time when you felt completely safe. | describe a time when you felt utterly stuck.*

◇ *your inner fire—describe a time when you did something bold and brave. | describe a time when you were so angry you saw red.*

◇ *your inner air—describe a time when you had an incredible breakthrough. | describe a time when overthinking got the better of you.*

◇ *your inner water—describe a time when you were so happy you were driven to tears. | describe a time when you felt like you were drowning in sadness.*

mother earth's help

mother earth doesn't just assist us with spells.

she wants to help us whenever she can, in whatever way she can, no matter who you are.

during my childhood, we had a family cat (who sadly passed away last week, as i go back to edit this) who would spend most of his days outside. there were plenty of nights when he never made it back home.

this, as you can probably imagine, was always extremely nerve-racking for me.

i would be sick to my stomach, imagining all the horrible things that could have happened to him—those worst-case scenarios that gnaw and gnaw. *what if he were lost at the other end of town? what if someone hurt him? what if someone stole him? even worse, what if he got run over by a car?*

back then, i didn't practice magic like i do now, but as a born nature lover and then-vegetarian (vegan now!), i still held a deep reverence for mother earth. i felt our connection, even though i couldn't explain it and would've probably sounded ridiculous trying to.

i'm not sure how long he had been gone, but one time, in my desperation, i went out to our backyard and asked mother earth—more specifically, the trees—to safely bring him back home to me.

as if on cue, the wind rustled their leaves, and he came running through the gate, crying out for me as if i had called him.

except calling his name didn't usually work.

but for some unknown reason, *this* had worked, and it worked almost every time after that, too. i didn't dare question it; i just remained extremely grateful.

when you need some extra help from mother earth, all you have to do is ask. do your best to be kind to her in return, even if that just means taking a few minutes out of your day to spend time in her presence. (that's all most good parents want, isn't it?)

grounding yourself

we, as humans, seem to have an endless list of demands and responsibilities, and because of that, our energy can sometimes get a little bit, uh . . . all over the place.

the way i see it, grounding is the act of energetically coming back home to yourself. the exercises below can help you become more present in your life as well as put you in the right headspace for spellwork.

go outside—if you're lucky enough to have your own outdoor space available, go to it. if not, you can go to your favorite local park, beach, or trail. take off your shoes and become reacquainted with the soil for a few minutes. let mother earth's energy recalibrate you. (this is called *earthing*.)

grow roots—can't go outside for whatever reason? no problem. go
someplace quiet and close your eyes. imagine roots growing from the
soles of your feet, burrowing through the floor and foundation into the
ground, planting you in place.

do something mindful—spend one-on-one time with your pet, relax in
front of an open window, watch a nature video on youtube, hold your
favorite plant/crystal, or drink a cup of herbal tea—spearmint is
my fave.

MAGICAL JOURNAL PROMPT: *write about something that makes you feel a
special connection to mother earth. it doesn't have to be super-magical; it can
be something small, like after-dinner walks around your neighborhood or even
just sitting underneath your favorite tree. what can you do to nurture this
connection, to expand on it even more?*

"white magic" vs. "black magic"

in the witchcraft community, you'll come across people who choose to use
the phrase "white magic" to mean "good magic" and the phrase "black
magic" to mean "evil magic."

that isn't okay.

it may seem inconsequential, but words hold a lot of weight. they
reflect and influence our society, and we live in one filled with a lot of
injustice. the racist implications of those phrases are not in line with my
personal *or* witchcraft ethics, and therefore i choose not to use them.

i discourage you from using them as well.

if you want to know how to describe what kind of magic someone practices, why not just ask them? i'm sure it would make for an interesting conversation!

be mindful of the words you say, not just during your spellwork, but at all times. no matter how well-meaning you are, you'll still get it wrong sometimes, but don't let that scare you—just recognize when you've caused harm, apologize, and do better (and don't just *say* you will).

witchcraft & gender

when someone says the word *witch*, you might automatically assume they're referring to a woman.

well, i'm here to tell you that people of all genders—because there are *way* more than just two!—can call themselves a witch. not just women, and certainly not just cis women.

when i said we *all* have magic within, i meant it.

in my opinion, being an ethical witch also means being an inclusive witch, and it's not very kind to leave so many of your fellow witches out of the conversation. doing so may make them feel like they don't belong in the community, and *everyone* deserves a sense of belonging.

be that safe space for every witch.

MAGICAL JOURNAL PROMPT: *in what ways can you be more inclusive in your everyday life, and how can you extend that to your magical practice?*

if you ever need some guidance,
no problem—

i'll help you interpret your tarot cards.

if you ever have a broken heart,
no problem—

i'll help you locate the right herbs.

if you ever need protection,
no problem—

i'll help you light your candles.

if you ever need defending,
no problem—

i'll help you find the words you need.

if you ever need a reality check,
no problem—

i'll help you be honest with yourself.

—as witches, we're all part of the same coven.

your witchcraft ethics

i can't tell you what kind of magic to make because i believe in the importance of free will, and it's *because* i believe in the importance of free will that i choose not to interfere with the free will of other people.

that means no love spells or curses.

you won't find either of those in this book.

> **these are both nuanced topics. in my opinion, there *are* ways to cast love spells without interfering with someone's free will (for example, casting a spell for the *type* of love you want, not for the love of a specific person—or better yet, casting a self-love spell). furthermore, marginalized people have historically used curses as a form of justice, so keep that in mind and don't hastily judge.**

as you'll probably notice, most of my spells and rituals have to do with things such as *self*-love, *self*-empowerment, *self*-worth, and bringing positive things into *my* life.

but cause and effect is a complex thing.

i recognize that it's possible that even those seemingly harmless spells could negatively impact others.

remember when i said that witches have the magic within to bring anything we want into existence? that comes with a *lot* of responsibility. while i can't feasibly control every little thing that happens as a result of my spells, i still try my best to do no harm by practicing magic with integrity and minimizing damage wherever i see potential for it.

before you cast a spell, carefully consider the potential impacts of it. in what ways could your spell affect you, positively *or* negatively? are there any neutral ways it could affect you? how about the ways it could affect other people? if relevant, you might also consider how it might affect mother earth. (i recommend getting out your magical journal to make some good, old-fashioned lists!)

after you reach your conclusion, decide if the spell is really worth it. (only *you* can do this.)

MAGICAL JOURNAL PROMPT: *now that you're almost ready to make some magic, what kind do you think you will make? write a list of your witchcraft ethics with plenty of room for growth. don't skip this part—it will be important soon!*

before making magic

next, i will ask you to cast your very first spell, but there are a few things i recommend doing beforehand. (this applies to all future spellwork as well.)

check in with your mind—if you're not thinking clearly, you may be more prone to forgetting steps or making mistakes. if you're feeling scattered, it might be a good idea to do a quick *grounding* exercise (see pages 32–33).

make a plan—write down all the steps to your spell in your magical journal beforehand, even if you didn't create the spell. this will help you execute the spell in the way only you can. for example, with a prewritten spell, you may want to personalize the affirmation or switch out some of the tools. leave room for notes after, too. these details show you what works for *you* and will help you with future spellwork.

set the tone—do what you need to create a private, distraction-free environment. unless you have notes for your spellwork on your phone—or it's an important part of the spell itself—turn on *do not disturb* and stash it somewhere you can't get to it. your instagram notifications can wait!

prepare your altar—the magical tools you'll be needing for your spell should all be within arm's reach. it's not the end of the world, but walking away from your altar to grab that "one more thing" three different times *might* eventually break the natural flow of your spell.

give yourself some peace of mind—you may want to *cleanse* the area of any energy that doesn't match the magic you're trying to make. you can do this by simply lighting a white candle and letting that be that. if you want to further *protect* the area from any unwanted energy that might flow in and potentially mess with your spellwork, go ahead and place a black tourmaline crystal on your altar.

make sure you're feeling your magic—spellwork should never be daunting or stressful, and it certainly shouldn't feel like an obligation. if the idea of it doesn't make you happy or at the very least content, then walk away from your altar and come back later. figure out what's not working, whether it's something personal or something about your spellwork that needs to change.

your first spell

congratulations—you've made it, witch! your very first spell is going to be all about the star of the show: you. the fact that you're deciding to go on this magical journey is kind of a big deal, so now you're officially going to give yourself permission to do so.

WHAT YOU'LL NEED

your list of magical ethics (see page 37)
a rose quartz crystal

DIRECTIONS

sit by your magical altar. place your list of magical ethics and your rose quartz crystal in front of you. begin by reading your list out loud, going point by point. don't just say these statements—*feel* them becoming part of your being.

next, hold the rose quartz crystal close to your heart and speak this affirmation: "i am allowed to be a witch. i am allowed to make my own magic, even if it doesn't look like anyone else's. i am allowed to make mistakes, and i am allowed to go easy on myself, for i am learning new things every day. most of all, i am allowed to have fun on this journey."

sit in silence with your rose quartz crystal for a few minutes. close your eyes and imagine the kind of witch you'd most like to be. go one step further and silently claim this witch as yourself, right now, in this very moment, not in some faraway and unknowable future.

when you're finished, say "so mote it be" to declare your spell as powerful and true.

MAGICAL JOURNAL PROMPT: *hopefully at this point you've already written down the details of your spell! if anything unexpected happened, or you decided to do something differently at the last minute, make sure you take note of that. then, make sure you explain how you* felt *while doing your spell. for example, did you feel like a witchy badass or like a total imposter? don't be afraid to be truthful!*

witchy labels

some people like to use specific labels to describe what kind of witch they are, such as a green witch (someone who works primarily with things like plants, flowers, and herbs to make their magic) or a sea witch (someone who works primarily with things such as sand, seawater, and seashells to make their magic).

meanwhile, some use more specific labels like crystal witch (someone who primarily uses crystals to make their magic), tarot witch (someone who primarily uses tarot cards to make their magic), or coffee witch (someone who primarily uses coffee to make their magic).

you don't have to label yourself right now.

you don't have to label yourself by the time you're done reading this book, either.

honestly, you don't have to label yourself *ever*, if you don't feel called to.

let yourself explore this new magical world first. if you *do* eventually decide to label yourself—perhaps because it helps you feel more connected to your practice—then that's awesome! just know that it's okay to change your mind later; it's okay to keep the label, too.

baby witch

in recent years, *baby witch* has become a label that new witches use to describe themselves—*you* don't have to, but i want to let you know that it's an option.

in my own experience, using the baby witch label can be very limiting and disempowering. i used that term for myself for *waaay* too long, mostly because i felt like i wasn't good enough or experienced enough to call myself a witch, even though i most definitely was after a certain point—experienced, that is; i was always good enough, and so are you.

when i dropped the "baby" part and finally just started calling myself a witch, i felt like i had finally stepped into my true magic, unapologetically and without shame . . . but, of course, everyone's different.

moral of the story: if it doesn't make you feel good, don't do it!

MAGICAL JOURNAL PROMPT: *do you like the idea of calling yourself a* baby witch, *or otherwise using a witchy label for yourself, either now or later? why or why not? i think it's helpful to take note of things like this, especially to see how your identity/beliefs develop over time.*

feeling confident yet?

it's *totally* normal not to feel confident when you've just started something.

i mean, you probably wouldn't feel confident on the first day of a new job, and starting your witchcraft journey is no different!

just like with a job, it may take a lot of time and practice to build up your self-esteem about magic. my advice? read as many witchcraft books as you possibly can (don't stop after this one!) and don't be afraid to ask tough questions and dig to seek answers. then experiment, experiment, experiment until you find your groove.

you'll get there eventually.

have a little patience with yourself.

something that used to cause me a lot of anxiety (and honestly still does, but mostly on behalf of new witches) was seeing other witches say, "that's not how you do *xyz*! *this* is how you do *xyz*." but you know what i came to realize? "this" is usually just their own personal preference— not fact.

for example, some witches like to do their manifestation rituals on the full moon, whereas some witches, like me, prefer to do their manifestation rituals on the new moon (more on these practices a little later).

who's wrong?

nobody.

we make our own magic whenever and however it feels right to *us*!

i promise you, as long as you're sticking to your witchcraft ethics (which you can revise at any time), there's no incorrect way to witch.

it's important to give space to other witches' opinions, as we all have a lot to learn from each other, but don't let them get in the way of practicing in a manner that feels true and authentic to you, okay?

MAGICAL JOURNAL PROMPT: *what's something that boosts your confidence? for example, you might like to put on lipstick or wear a certain article of clothing. see if you can incorporate that into your spellwork to help you feel more self-assured.*

when they're staring off into space
& unusually quiet,

you don't have to worry that
they're angry, sad, or annoyed.

they're just trying to listen
for the strings of their heartsong.

—*the most beautiful melody in the world.*

part ii

your intuition

"what's intuition?"

has there ever been a time when you knew something without actually *knowing* it? a gut feeling you couldn't shake no matter how hard you tried, even though there was no "logical" reason behind it? just an unexplainable knowing with no fear?

that right there is your *intuition*, witch, and it can show up as:

◆ thinking about someone you know and getting a text/call from them a few minutes later.

◆ canceling plans because something doesn't feel quite right, and later finding out that something less than ideal happened en route (like a traffic delay or a car accident) or where you were supposed to be (like an argument or the appearance of someone you *definitely* didn't want to see).

◆ buying a book because you can sense you're supposed to read it, and it changes your life.

◆ circling an answer on a test not because you know it to be correct but because something in you told you it is. it ends up being right.

◆ knowing that your partner is cheating on you even though there are no typical signs, and then something—or someone—confirms it for you.

and that's just the beginning.

experiences like this show you that you know *way* more than you think you do.

they also show you how imperative it is to not only listen to yourself but to wholeheartedly trust yourself.

while some of the intuitive hits you get might just be cool little reminders that your intuition is on point (like the anticipated text or call), much of the time, your intuition acts as your inner guide, pulling you toward what's good for you and pushing you away from what isn't.

we all have intuition, but sadly, not many people know how to tap into theirs or understand what it's trying to tell them. and it's no wonder—it isn't exactly a skill that's widely taught. we also live in a society where we're supposed to follow the rules, and intuition doesn't work like that.

some witches practice something called divination to help them get more in touch with their inner wisdom, and that's what i'm going to teach you next!

MAGICAL JOURNAL PROMPT: *reflect on a time when you got an intuitive hunch about something. what was it like? maybe you just knew something. maybe you heard something, saw something, felt something, or even smelled something. (that last one may sound funny, but it's real. i tend to get overcome by people's scents just before finding out they've passed.) describe your own unique intuition in as much detail as possible so you can begin to understand it a little better.*

whenever you have an intuitive hunch in the future, keep track of it in your magical journal, even if it doesn't immediately appear to be correct. it very well could come true later, and you'll definitely want to go back and see how right you were!

47

"um, okay, but what's divination?"

divination is the practice of using tools such as tarot cards, oracle cards, and pendulums to receive magical messages.

(yes, crystal balls are sometimes used, too!)

just like portrayals of witches are highly dramatized in the media, portrayals of divination tend to be, too. no, it's not going to start storming the second you take out your box of tarot cards (though it would be cool if it did), and no, you're probably not going to predict someone's tragic and untimely death.

there *is* a small grain of truth to these depictions, though: depending on how you choose to use them, divination tools can give you a glimpse into your future.

predicting stuff isn't the *only* thing they can do, however.

most of the time, i like to use divination as a means of gaining deep, magical insight about my life and goals—to self-reflect on where i've been, to get clear on where exactly i am now in my journey, and to find some guidance about my path moving forward.

"wait. i thought you had to be psychic to use tarot cards & stuff?"

i can see why you would think that.

growing up, my mom collected tarot cards and oracle cards filled with beautiful beings like angels and faeries. i loved to sit down and go through them, admiring the artwork and dreaming that i could one day be a card reader . . .

but that's as far as it went for many years.

i didn't even try to learn how to read them because i, like so many people, was under the impression that i had to have some innate psychic gift in order to accurately glean their wisdom, and an innate psychic gift i did not possess.

or so i thought.

eventually, i learned that just like anyone can be a witch, *anyone* can dabble in the art of divination if they want to, so now i do—every single day of my life. (just to clarify: you do *not* have to be a witch in order to do divination, or vice versa. anyone can. however, it's a very popular practice among today's witches.)

to read the cards, all you need is one thing: your intuition. as you know by now, this is something everyone has.

some people might even say intuition *is* an innate psychic gift. (i'm some people.)

in my opinion, when you ask a question of your tarot cards (or your other divination tools), you're the one who actually provides the answer— anything they say comes right from within you. you may not *think* you know those things, but you do, even if it's deep, deep, deep down on a subconscious level. all your tools do is translate it in a way you can better understand.

MAGICAL JOURNAL PROMPT: *what's something you've always wanted to do, but you've convinced yourself you're not capable of doing it? how might your own self-limiting beliefs be holding you back, not just in terms of divination, but in other areas of your witchcraft practice as well?*

telling the future

before you even so much as think about touching a divination tool, it's important for you to understand something: nothing—and while we're at it, no *one*—can predict your future with complete and 100% certainty.

what divination tools *can* do is show you what there's potential for.

it's all about *possibilities*.

personally, i don't think my fate is set in stone.

it's constantly being shaped by my thoughts, decisions, and actions; therefore, it's ever-changing. divination tools can only predict so much based on what i'm thinking, deciding, and doing at this very moment.

and if i get an answer i don't like, i do whatever i can to change it, practically and/or magically.

because like i said, i am never powerless.

i am power*ful*.

and so are you, witch.

MAGICAL JOURNAL PROMPT: *do you think you write your life story as you go, or do you think a higher force has already written your story for you? is it maybe a little bit of both?*

i have this morning ritual
where i open my blinds

& imagine
the sky asking me,

"what will you make of today?"

instead of responding,
all i can do is smile because

i can make anything i want.
i can even remake myself, if i want.

—*forever choosing my own adventure.*

your divination ethics

we've already talked about your ethics regarding your overall witchcraft
practice. now we're going to get specific and talk about your ethics
regarding your divination practice.

i can't tell you what kind of witchcraft ethics to have, and i can't tell
you what kind of divination ethics to have, either.

that's up to you, as it should be!

however, i will give you a little guidance, which you can either take or
leave. i just ask that you stop and consider it carefully. divination can be

helpful and even fun at times, but it can also be very serious and should always be approached as such.

in this book, i'll be teaching you how to do divination for yourself and about yourself. (others may be brought up in your readings, but i suggest you handle it in a noninvasive way.) personally, i think that's the best place to start. if you're interested, you can do divination for other people once you get some practice in.

with that said, i do strongly caution you against doing readings about others unless they give you explicit permission to do so.

how would you feel if someone did a reading about your personal matters without telling you? uncomfortable, i'm sure. maybe even totally violated, depending on what type of information they are seeking. keep that in mind and treat others the way you would want to be treated.

finally, i strongly caution you against asking overly serious questions about others (and even yourself), especially ones that could potentially have devastating or anxiety-inducing answers, such as about matters like health, pregnancy, legal issues, or death.

remember: just because you *can* ask certain things doesn't mean you *should*.

i won't pretend i'm perfect. i've made a lot of mistakes to get to where i am. when i didn't know any better, i asked my cards questions i probably shouldn't have. i even did spells i wouldn't do now—nothing disgraceful, just not in line with who i am today. i've taken those situations and turned them into lessons that strengthen my morals moving forward.

MAGICAL JOURNAL PROMPT: *write a list of your divination ethics. make sure to tab it so you can go back to it whenever you need a reminder or to revise things you've changed your mind about.*

tarot cards

there's some debate on where tarot originated, but most people believe it started as an italian playing card game back in the 1400s, eventually transforming into the divination tool we all know and love today.

> *cartomancy* is the practice of using cards for divination.

when you think of tarot, the first thing you think of is probably the rider-waite-smith tarot deck.

the rider-waite-smith deck was first published in the early 1900s and is considered by many to be the traditional deck. it's also the most popular among witches and other tarot practitioners. in fact, most seventy-eight-card tarot decks you'll find on shelves at stores like target, barnes & noble, and your local witchcraft shop are reinterpretations of it!

because of the way tarot (and more specifically, the rider-waite-smith deck) has been showcased in all forms of media—books, tv, movies, even music—most people are familiar with iconic cards such as death, the devil, and the lovers, even if they don't know exactly what they mean.

tarot misconceptions

tarot has had an undeniable impact on media and pop culture, yet
most people only know a few surface-level things about it. much of that
knowledge is misinformation that scares them away from getting their own
deck and learning how to use it.

so let's clear some things up:

◆ you do not have to be given your first tarot deck as a gift, and it's
  definitely not "bad luck" to buy your own. unless the gifter knows you
  really well, i encourage you to do your own deck shopping—that way,
  you can make sure you get one you really connect with!

◆ tarot cards are symbolic in their meanings. if you pull the devil card,
  the literal devil isn't going to rise from the fiery pits of hell to get you.
  more likely, it points toward a toxic person (which can sometimes be
  you) or pattern present in your life.

◆ you're allowed to read for yourself; in fact, it's amazing practice for if/
  when you want to read for other people. just try not to be too biased in
  your interpretations since the topic—*you*—is so personal! (it happens
  to the best of us.)

◆ you don't need to memorize the card meanings. there isn't going to
  be a quiz you either pass or fail. if you try to commit them to memory,
  you could end up stressing yourself out too much to have an accurate
  reading. just try to have a good grasp on the general vibe of the card so
  you have a starting point for your intuitive interpretations, even if that
  means consulting a guidebook here and there.

- with that said, there is no "right" way or "wrong" way to read the cards, so don't let anyone try to tell you otherwise. everyone's intuition is going to interpret stuff differently. your unique perspective is what makes your readings so special.

- you don't have to read using reversed cards (aka upside-down cards), but honestly, they aren't as bad as some people make them out to be. a lot of the time, they just show you something that you need to work on or overcome, which can be some pretty important information to know!

MAGICAL JOURNAL PROMPT: *what's your biggest fear when it comes to learning to read tarot? as you write, imagine the fear leaving your body, running through your pen, and being disposed of on the page.*

tarot structure

tarot has a structured seventy-eight-card system (it's not as scary as it sounds, i swear!) and some modern interpretations choose to include more cards. this system is split into two defined parts: the major arcana and the minor arcana.

the major arcana—makes up the first twenty-two cards (#0–21). they tend to represent big themes in your life—think *major*, life-defining lessons, people, and events. these are the cards you want to pay the most attention to in a reading because they'll point toward anything super-pressing that might be affecting your life.

the minor arcana—makes up the remaining fifty-six cards. split into four suits (cups, pentacles, swords, and wands), these cards represent the *minor*, everyday things you might deal with. each suit also contains a four-card court (page, knight, queen, and king), which can represent people/personalities (you or others) that may come into play. the minor arcana cards hold less weight than the major arcana cards, but small things have the potential to snowball into something huge, so do pay attention—you could easily avoid some drama!

tarot meanings

soon, i'm going to provide you with a list of tarot card meanings in the form of easy-to-remember phrases. you don't have to read them straight through—think of them more as a reference. (disclaimer: there are *many* ways to look at the cards. these are just my own personal distillations.)

they are, by no means, intended as the be-all, end-all. there's a lot more to tarot meanings than you'll find in this book, but this is a great place to start if you're feeling overwhelmed. and if you are, i totally get it! seventy-eight cards are a *lot* to take in. it took me years to become familiar with each and every one of them. i still struggle sometimes, especially with the court cards. (ugh.)

other people's meanings aren't the most important thing to take into consideration, anyway. your intuitive interpretations are.

when you pull a card, read it with your gut first. take in the colors, the symbols, the animals, the people. what does it mean to *you*? once you have that down, take a glimpse at my meaning and see if you can put your interpretation into that context.

if you can't, then stand by your intuitive interpretation. you hold all the knowledge, so you're probably trying to tell yourself something only you can get.

picking a tarot deck

before you can begin, make sure you get yourself a tarot deck. choosing a deck—let alone your first one—can be a stressful experience. there are already countless in existence, and there are more and more coming out every single year. how is a witch supposed to choose?!

here are a few things for you to consider:

- ◆ you may want to start with the traditional deck: the rider-waite-smith. there are a few different versions to choose from, such as *radiant rider-waite tarot* or *tarot vintage*. once you learn how to read with those cards, you can read most seventy-eight-card decks with ease.

- ◆ decks can be found via well-known places like amazon and barnes & noble, but not all decks are traditionally published or widely available. use google or search tarot-related tags on social media to see if you can find interesting indie ones. better yet, poke through your local witchcraft store and see what they have!

- ◆ most decks you'll find are illustrated. some are hyperrealistic, others cartoonish, and some fall somewhere in-between. some are pastel; some are moody. take time to think about what kind of art style you prefer.

◆ some decks feature people or animals. some feature witches, goddesses, faeries, angels, dragons, or unicorns. some feature crystals or plants or even characters from pop culture. the list goes on and on and on. which theme do you think *you* would connect with the most?

◆ you may come across a deck you feel an unexplainable pull toward, even though you don't necessarily connect with the art style or the theme. as always, trust your intuition—it's probably telling you that you'll connect with it in less obvious ways.

once you land on a deck, you'll definitely want to magically cleanse it, because who *knows* how many hands it's been in before it got to you. you can do this with the usual tools we've already gone over, or you can just knock on the top of the deck three times. (three is a super-magical number in witchcraft, so witches often do magical things in groups of three.)

MAGICAL JOURNAL PROMPT: *which tarot deck did you choose as your first? explain what drew you to it and your initial impressions of it.*

the major arcana meanings

the major arcana tells the story of the fool's journey (card 0). these cards reveal the big blessings, the almost-impossible challenges, and everything else we go through in life that shapes us, from beginning to end.

0: the fool—you're taking the first step on a grand new adventure (upright) | you might be scared to start something; put fear aside and take the leap! (reversed)

1: the magician—you're manifesting your dreams and goals (upright) | your lack of self-belief is blocking your success (reversed)

2: the high priestess—your intuition is spot-on in this situation (upright) | you're ignoring your inner wisdom to your own detriment (reversed)

3: the empress—you're flourishing in so many beautiful ways, especially creatively (upright) | you aren't nurturing yourself enough (reversed)

4: the emperor—you've got everything under control (upright) | it's time to take back your power, witch (reversed)

5: the hierophant—you might find value in following tradition (upright) | screw tradition and do things your own way (reversed)

6: the lovers—you have an important choice to make involving your personal desires (upright) | your heart may be leading you astray (reversed)

7: the chariot—your determination is pulling you forward (upright) | your lack of motivation is halting your progress (reversed)

8: strength—you're strong enough to do anything (upright) | don't doubt your inner strength so much, lovely (reversed)

9: the hermit—look within for guidance (upright) | you're spending a little too much time alone with your own thoughts (reversed)

10: wheel of fortune—you're having an amazing stroke of luck (upright) | don't let bad luck get you down; it will all come back around (reversed)

11: justice—you're being rewarded for sticking to your morals (upright) | you may need to face the consequences of your own actions (reversed)

12: the hanged man—you're resting between big chapters (upright) | your impatience is making things so much worse than they need to be (reversed)

13: death—this version of yourself is over and it's for the best (upright) | you're hanging on to an old version of yourself that no longer serves you (reversed)

14: temperance—you're blissfully balanced (upright) | you need to create a little more harmony in your life, bestie (reversed)

15: the devil—there's a toxic person or pattern in your life (upright) | do something about that toxic person/pattern before the damage gets too severe (reversed)

16: the tower—your life is going to be turned upside down (upright) | you're fighting necessary change and causing yourself more pain (reversed)

17: the star—your life is about to get *sooo* much better (upright) | keep having faith and keep going (reversed)

18: the moon—something is about to come to light, causing all kinds of realizations (upright) | despite your fears, it's okay to be exposed and vulnerable (reversed)

19: the sun—you're about to have very good reason to be a happy-go-lucky witch (upright) | you're not letting yourself do what gives you joy (reversed)

20: judgement—you're feeling called to step up and do something huge and unexpected (upright) | you're ignoring the call because you fail to see how amazing it'll be (reversed)

21: the world—you're celebrating a long-awaited accomplishment (upright) | you're afraid to move on to the next grand adventure, but there's nothing to fear (reversed)

the minor arcana
cups suit meanings

the first minor arcana suit we'll look at is the cups, which is associated with the element of water. these cards speak to your experiences with emotions, intuition, and inspiration. many of them have to do with relationships, romantic or otherwise.

ace of cups—you're being blessed with a new feeling or connection that has potential to be expanded upon (upright) | why aren't you doing anything to take this thing to the next level? (reversed)

two of cups—you can trust this deep, loving connection with someone (upright) | there may be a rough patch in a relationship, so give it some extra tlc (reversed)

three of cups—your friend group is absolutely thriving (upright) | oops—friendship fallout on the way! see if you can salvage the good (reversed)

four of cups—you're becoming bored with everyone and everything (upright) | your stagnancy is officially negatively impacting your emotional well-being—change it up asap! (reversed)

five of cups—you're grieving and it's making you blind to your other blessings (upright) | it's *been* time to move on (reversed)

six of cups—you're feeling delightfully nostalgic (upright) | you need to realize that there's a difference between reminiscing and being stuck in the past (reversed)

seven of cups—you have so many options that speak to your heart (upright) | you're overwhelmed by the choices—pick what *feels* right! (reversed)

eight of cups—you're leaving something that no longer fulfills you (upright) | you refuse to walk away even though things probably won't change (reversed)

nine of cups—you have *so* much to be thankful for (upright) | you might be acting a little bit ungrateful (reversed)

ten of cups—you're living your happiest life (upright) | you're living the dream, but it doesn't really feel like it's enough anymore (reversed)

page of cups—the daydreamer who gets attached to a new fictional character every week (upright) | someone who's a tad emotionally immature (reversed)

knight of cups—the charming and romantic type who follows their every heartcall (upright) | a person who *seems* charming and romantic until you get to know the real them (reversed)

queen of cups—the typical empath who takes care of everyone (upright) | a people-pleaser who needs to focus on their own feelings for a change (reversed)

king of cups—someone who's balanced and mature (upright) | an emotionally manipulative person (reversed)

the minor arcana
pentacles suit meanings

next up is the pentacles suit, which is related to the element of earth. these cards have to do with things such as stability, nature, and prosperity. love it or hate it (and there are plenty of reasons to hate it), the material world we live in has a constant impact on us!

ace of pentacles—you've been given a material opportunity with tons of potential (upright) | you were given that potential, only to throw it away (reversed)

two of pentacles—you're trying to balance work, life, and other responsibilities (upright) | you're not prioritizing the right stuff (reversed)

three of pentacles—you're working with and learning from others (upright) | you'll need to start playing nice with others in order to accomplish anything (reversed)

four of pentacles—you're feeling financially stable (upright) | you're *so* financially stable that you're scared to spend a dime (reversed)

five of pentacles—you might be experiencing some sort of lack or fear of lack (upright) | you're being given a helping hand, so take it (reversed)

six of pentacles—you're giving (or receiving) a generous gift (upright) | you may experience a lack of charity (reversed)

seven of pentacles—you're growing something to see what it flourishes into (upright) | you haven't seen results yet and you're rightfully frustrated (reversed)

eight of pentacles—you've been working away to make sure you achieve your goals (upright) | you're too caught up in the tiny details to get anything done (reversed)

nine of pentacles—you're a self-made success and you know it (upright) | you aren't enjoying your success enough (reversed)

ten of pentacles—you've reached your ultimate financial goal (upright) | you reached your ultimate financial goal but still don't feel satisfied— why? (reversed)

page of pentacles—a person who's figuring out their life and career (upright) | someone who has no direction or prospects (reversed)

knight of pentacles—someone who makes smart, deliberate moves toward their goals (upright) | the one who's afraid to try new things and take healthy risks (reversed)

queen of pentacles—the one who flawlessly manages their schedule and everyone else's (upright) | someone who's overworked and overburdened (reversed)

king of pentacles—the steadfast success who makes sure everyone around them has what they need (upright) | someone who's greedy af (reversed)

the minor arcana
swords suit meanings

now for the swords suit. these cards represent the element of air. the themes of this suit are intellect, ideas, and communication. some of the most "reality check"–type cards appear here, so a lot of people hate it, but you know what? sometimes those reality checks are *needed*.

ace of swords—you have an idea with tons of potential (upright) | you're deciding not to follow it through (reversed)

two of swords—you're making a choice between two directions (upright) | stop pretending you don't know what you want to do (reversed)

three of swords—your heart is broken (upright) | you've been focused on the rain clouds a little too long; time to get dry and move on, witch-friend (reversed)

four of swords—you need to rest your body and your mind (upright) | you refused to recharge, so your body and mind decided to take a break for you (reversed)

five of swords—you may have won the debate, but you lost a lot of respect in the process (upright) | put aside your ego and fix what you broke (reversed)

six of swords—you're departing from a difficult situation to find healing (upright) | you're carrying too much baggage to properly move on (reversed)

seven of swords—you have to be sneaky to get what you deserve sometimes (upright) | selfishness =/= self-care (reversed)

eight of swords—you feel trapped (upright) | you're not as helpless as you claim to be—free yourself asap (reversed)

nine of swords—you're very anxious about something (upright) | you've run so far away with your worries that it's affecting your reality (reversed)

ten of swords—you've been betrayed (upright) | pick yourself back up and dress your wounds (reversed)

page of swords—that person who loves to learn and texts you a new fun fact every day (upright) | the type that would spread rumors or misinformation (reversed)

knight of swords—a person who isn't afraid to chase after their dreams (upright) | someone who does things without thinking of the consequences (reversed)

queen of swords—someone who isn't afraid to speak their truth (upright) | a person who cuts others down with their words (reversed)

king of swords—the smartest person you know (upright) | someone who doesn't take anyone's feelings into account when making decisions (reversed)

the minor arcana
wands suit meanings

finally, we have the wands suit! this suit is related to the element of fire. here, you'll find cards that have to do with things like passion, creativity, and energy. (as a creative person, i find that the wands cards tend to show up for me *a lot.*)

ace of wands—you're having a burst of creativity with potential (upright) | you're not following where your passion is trying to lead you (reversed)

two of wands—you're putting some plans into motion (upright) | you're like, "i want to do the thing, but idk where to start" (reversed)

three of wands—you're about to see the outcome of all your hard work (upright) | you're not seeing the results you expected by now—get back to the planning board! (reversed)

four of wands—you're feeling comfortable and at home with the people around you (upright) | you aren't feeling supported or understood (reversed)

five of wands—you're in an argument that's gotten too heated (upright) | this can't be solved until everyone calms tf down (reversed)

six of wands—you're finally getting the recognition you deserve (upright) | you shouldn't be scared to be the center of attention—you've earned it! (reversed)

seven of wands—you may have to defend yourself against people praying for your downfall (upright) | you're letting your haters get to you too much (reversed)

eight of wands—you should expect some progress, like, now (upright) | you aren't happy with the speed of things (reversed)

nine of wands—you're still standing after an exhausting challenge (upright) | don't give up yet, okay? (reversed)

ten of wands—you're taking on a lot, but you're almost done (upright) | you burned yourself out by carrying too much (reversed)

page of wands—that person who's passionate about something new every day (upright) | a person who can't find their lust for life (reversed)

knight of wands—someone who charges toward every desire they have (upright) | the wild and reckless type (reversed)

queen of wands—that person who isn't afraid to shine brightly (upright) | someone who needs to tap into their confidence (reversed)

king of wands—the one who does what they love and empowers everyone else to do the same (upright) | a temperamental and angry person who scares others (reversed)

your first tarot reading

once you find a tarot deck you resonate with and you've familiarized yourself a little with the cards, it's time to do your first reading! (you've got this!)

WHAT YOU'LL NEED
a purple candle in a holder
an amethyst crystal
a lighter or match
your deck
your magical journal
a writing utensil

DIRECTIONS

on your altar, arrange your purple candle and amethyst crystal however you'd like. as you light your candle, say, "i open myself to receive messages from my intuition. i trust my inner wisdom without fear or hesitation, for it would never tell me something i don't already know or can't handle."

now, take your deck and shuffle it for a few moments or until you're satisfied that the cards are mixed up enough.

it may feel a little silly, but i want you to introduce yourself to your deck and let it know that you're going to ask some questions. this is called a deck interview, which can be done before using any new deck you get.

for each of the three prompts below, hold your deck in between both your hands and ask your question. shuffle, then pull a card. (*always* prompt your deck before pulling a card; otherwise, you'll just get a random message with no context, which is super-unhelpful.)

◆ "now that you know who i am, who are you? describe yourself with one card."

◆ "how can i best connect with you?"

◆ "if you could give me any piece of advice right now, what would it be?"

as you move through each of these questions, make sure you write down the questions as well as your interpretations of the deck's answers in your magical journal. when you're finished with your reading, thank your deck for giving you its time and energy, then let your candle either burn down or extinguish it and use it for your next reading.

daily tarot practice

if you want to learn tarot, a great way to become familiar with the cards is to do a daily one-card pull. i like to go over to my altar after i wake up and pull one to help set the tone for my day.

you can ask whatever question you'd like, but here are some questions/prompts i have in my rotation:

◆ which intention would best serve me?

◆ what is the energy/theme of my day?

◆ how can i kick ass and meet goals?

come back to your altar before you go to sleep and contemplate how this message played out. this way, over time, you'll learn what each card means for *you*, making your future readings that much more accurate!

challenge: try pulling two cards to answer a single question/prompt, using your own common sense and intuitive creativity to combine their meanings. for example, let's say you pull the tower and nine of cups for your intention. i'd interpret this as, *when it seems like everything is going awry, take a moment to remember how many blessings you still have left.*

tarot spread to remind you of your purpose

when you feel a little lost in life, do this three-card spread to help guide you out of the woods. interpret each card individually and then see if you can find any connections across the cards—not just in their meanings, but in their illustrations and symbols. what do they tell you? some symbols have common meanings you can find with a quick search, but your own personal associations are often much more powerful.

* ⁕ CARD SPREAD ⁕ *

CARD 1	CARD 2	CARD 3
what is my purpose?	which action can i take right now in order to live up to my fullest potential?	a message to empower me on my current path.

MAGICAL JOURNAL PROMPT: *have you ever thought about what your purpose could be? is it different than the card you pulled? keep in mind that you can have more than one. also, your purpose might not be something obvious, like* helping others *or* being a parent. *sometimes your purpose can be something simple such as* being happy, *which is just as valid.*

other ways to use tarot cards

daily magic—for this, you're going to purposely pick a tarot card to represent the energy you want to embody that day. for example, if you want to have a relaxing and restful day off, try displaying the four of swords on your altar.

journaling—tarot cards can be used as journaling prompts, too. to do this, ask your deck to give you a random card, or alternatively, you can purposely pick a card that you want to write about. once you have your card, explore what it means to you and how it relates to your life or current situation. is there any guidance you can take away from this card?

> **try pulling a tarot card to help inspire some of your answers to the magical journal prompts in this book.**

spellwork—i've been known to incorporate tarot cards into my spellwork. the way i see it, each card holds the energy of its unique meaning, and you can invite that energy into your spell in the same way you would with candles, herbs, and crystals. next, i'll show you how to do a spell for confidence using tarot!

tarot spell for self-confidence

this spell is perfect whenever you need a confidence boost, whether it's for a specific occasion (like giving a presentation, standing up to someone, or doing anything that intimidates you) or just in general!

WHAT YOU'LL NEED
the queen of wands tarot card
a red candle in a holder
a lighter or match
a tiger's-eye crystal
three cinnamon sticks

DIRECTIONS

hold your queen of wands card up to eye level and affirm, "this is who i am: a confident badass." place it down flat in the middle of the spellwork area on your altar.

on top of the card, place your red candle. as you light it, say, "i am a confident and *strong* badass."

placing the tiger's-eye crystal next to or in front of your candle, say, "i am a confident, strong, and *courageous* badass."

finally, take your three cinnamon sticks and creatively place them in/around the other components of your spell, such as bordering it in a triangle shape, if space allows. as you place your third and last cinnamon stick, say, "i am a confident, strong, and courageous badass now and always. so mote it be."

let your candle burn down or extinguish it and use it for a future confidence spell.

you may also choose to carry the crystal with you or make it into a bracelet/ necklace so it can inspire confidence on the go!

she walks with her head held high
knowing that she has
tiger's-eye dangling from her wrist
& fire raging inside of her belly.

—*better watch out for the witch.*

oracle cards

one of the questions i'm asked most is, "hey amanda, what's the difference between tarot cards and oracle cards?"

the answer is *way* less complicated than you probably think.

by now, you already know that most tarot decks have a structured seventy-eight-card system based on the traditional rider-waite-smith tarot deck. in other words, when you pick up any tarot deck, you pretty much know what you're going to get, adjusted for some artistic license.

that's not the case with oracle decks.

when i created the *believe in your own magic* oracle deck, i didn't abide by any rules. it's based on my women are some kind of magic poetry series, but that was only a guide i followed as closely or as loosely as i wanted. the theme, the number of cards, the card names, the card meanings, the structure—that was all me. there was no traditional oracle deck to reference because there *isn't* one.

my point: each oracle deck in existence is unique. i can't give you meanings because those can only be found in each deck's individual guidebook.

i find that there's a difference in the type of messages you get from tarot cards versus oracle cards, too. tarot decks tend to have more mundane and practical meanings (*not* a bad thing), whereas oracle decks usually speak more to your inner world—gentle guidance, thought-provoking messages, positive affirmations.

i use and love both kinds of decks, and i think there's room for both in a witch's life.

as with your first tarot deck, you'll want to search around until you find an oracle deck you intuitively connect with. you'll also want to write about why you chose it, cleanse it, and conduct a deck interview with it (see page 71—yep, same questions and everything!). since oracle card meanings tend to be less direct, you might have to be a little creative with your interpretations!

MAGICAL JOURNAL PROMPT: *some people prefer tarot decks over oracle decks, while some prefer oracle decks over tarot decks. once you've had a chance to use your oracle deck, write about which kind of deck you prefer and why. know that you don't have to choose one over the other—some kinds of decks are just better suited for certain types of readings, which is something else you can explore for yourself in your answer.*

oracle spread to check in with yourself

just like you check in on the people in your life, you should take the time to check in on yourself, too. in case no one has ever told you this before: *your well-being is just as important as the well-being of those you love.* with that said, let's see how you've been tending to yourself and how you can better care for yourself moving forward with this simple three-card spread.

⁎ ⁎ **CARD SPREAD** ⁎ ⁎

CARD 1	*CARD 2*	*CARD 3*
the part of myself i've been prioritizing lately.	the part of myself i've been neglecting.	the best way to show the neglected part of myself more love.

MAGICAL JOURNAL PROMPT: *over the next few days, find a way to heed card 3's advice and take the time to write about your experience. how do you think this has benefited you in the short term? do you think you'll try this self-care technique again in the future?*

you can use your oracle cards in all the same ways you use your tarot cards. you can also use your oracle cards in your tarot readings, so feel free to mix and match decks if you want to shake things up a little. personally, i like to use oracle cards at the end of tarot readings for a little dose of self-encouragement or self-empowerment—that way, the reading always ends on an inspiring note, which is helpful for those more emotionally difficult readings.

daily oracle card affirmation ritual

when you get a new oracle deck, you'll want to pull a card every day until you're familiar with them all. this is *especially* important since every oracle deck is different and will ultimately give you a totally new experience. you may find that you form a stronger relationship with the cards using this hands-on daily affirmation ritual.

WHAT YOU'LL NEED
an oracle deck
your magical journal
a writing utensil
a piece of scrap paper

DIRECTIONS

shuffle your oracle deck while asking the question, "which affirmation would be most helpful to me today?"

once you have your card, i want you to display it on your magical altar and really take in the illustration as well as the guidebook meaning. what energy does this card give off? what intuitive messages do you get when you look at it? be sure to write down any words or phrases that come to mind in your magical journal.

next, i want you to use those notes to craft a sentence-long affirmation.

if you don't know what to write, start with the phrase, "i am _____." and fill in the blank. for example, "i am worthy of all the things i want," "i am shining my light for everyone to see," or "i am willing to practice forgiveness for my own peace of mind."

once you have your final affirmation, write it down on a piece of scrap paper and find a place to display it on your altar, preferably next to your oracle card pull.

repeat this affirmation aloud to yourself and say, "so mote it be."

come back to your altar at least two more times that day and repeat this affirmation to yourself so you won't forget it. if that's not possible because of work or school (or, if you're like me, any number of target or dunkin' runs), you can also take a picture of it and set it as the lock screen on your phone.

pendulums

before you know what they are, pendulums can seem pretty unassuming. after all, they usually resemble necklaces: a long chain with some sort of charm at the end.

in fact, some witches—like me—take off their necklace and use it as a pendulum in a pinch. (what can i say? convenience is *everything*.)

most people would probably be surprised to learn that pendulum dowsing—aka using a pendulum for divination—is not only an ancient practice but a very powerful divination method, as the answers you'll receive are very straightforward.

using a pendulum is effortless. you just have to ask a question and wait for the pendulum to swing this way or that. which answer will it be: yes, no, or maybe?

whichever answer you get, it will be certain to confirm your inner wisdom.

picking a pendulum

like i said earlier, pendulums are usually long chains with charms at the end. the charm can be made from any number of materials, such as wood, metal, or resin. you can even find acorn or seashell pendulums.

most commonly, though, it will be a crystal.

for divination purposes, i highly recommend you get your hands on an amethyst pendulum; as you know, it has properties that help support your intuition, so you can see why it's an overall sound choice.

however, *any* crystal you vibe with will likely make for a good one.

i'm sure you already know this by now, but the first thing you should do when you get your pendulum is cleanse it. after, take out your magical journal and write about why you picked it, then get ready to do the pendulum version of a deck interview, which i'll guide you through next!

> don't have access to a pendulum? use a necklace with a pendant or even a string with a paper clip tied to the end instead.

your first pendulum session

okay, now that you have your pendulum, you're probably eager to use it!

WHAT YOU'LL NEED
a clear quartz crystal
your pendulum
your magical journal
a writing utensil

DIRECTIONS

first, place your clear quartz crystal down on your altar while saying this affirmation: "i offer myself clear and enlightening answers during this pendulum session."

sit in such a way that you can comfortably rest your elbow on your altar, because your forearm needs to be raised and steady. keep in mind that you might get tired in this position, and it's okay to take breaks whenever you need to.

next, using your dominant hand, pinch the charmless end of your pendulum chain between your index and thumb. let any leftover chain rest between your other fingers and palm. the charmed end should dangle freely.

now you're going to program your pendulum.

this is where you teach your pendulum which way to swing to indicate yes, no, and maybe. go through each one, doing the motion you prefer to represent each answer. choose whatever makes the most sense to you.

here's what i do: a clockwise circle for yes, a counterclockwise circle for no, and a horizontal sway for maybe.

after you program it, test it. ask some yes/no questions you already know the answers to, like, "is my name _____?" "am i __ years old?" or "do i live in (town/state/country)?" (switch it up and ask questions you know to be false, too, so you can fully test its accuracy.)

the movements may take a while to start, or they might only be slight, so pay close attention!

take note of everything that happens in your magical journal. don't become too disheartened if your pendulum doesn't seem to be working correctly, or if it gives confusing or contradictory answers. sometimes you just have to work with it a little more so it can become attuned to your energy and intuition.

taking it further with your pendulum

with your first pendulum session behind you, you're probably saying, "now what?"

there are so many ways you can work with your pendulum on the regular, but here are a few you might like to try!

double-check yourself—sometimes we get intuitive tugs, but we aren't fully confident in the way we interpret them. when in doubt, pull out your trusty pendulum and ask it if you're interpreting things correctly, making sure you voice your interpretation clearly. if you get a "no" answer, then ask your pendulum follow-up questions until you get to the bottom of it.

tarot/oracle card readings—i absolutely love to use my pendulum in my tarot and oracle card readings. as i interpret each card, i ask my pendulum if i'm on the right track. if i get a yes, then yay, but if i get a no, then i know i need to spend a little more time tuning in to my unique intuition, even if it means straying from the usual card meaning.

make decisions—within *reason*, of course. you should never do something risky just because your pendulum told you to (or your tarot and oracle cards, for that matter). always use a combination of intuition and logic just to be safe. you can start by using your pendulum to help you with small/inconsequential decisions. for example, i sometimes pull out my pendulum when my spouse and i are trying to decide what to have for dinner, because we're both really indecisive people. i go through each option and ask, "should we have _____?" until we get a yes. works like a charm every time.

MAGICAL JOURNAL PROMPT: *get some pendulum practice in by picking an afternoon to bring your pendulum with you everywhere. take it out whenever you have an everyday choice to make—which route to take, which response to text back, which picture/video to post on social media. (you may have to ignore some weird looks from people, but who cares?) come back at the end of the day and write about your experience.*

other divination methods

maybe you can't get your hands on a deck or a pendulum, or maybe you just don't vibe with them. don't sweat it. here are some divination methods that use tools that are easier to come by, and one that doesn't require tools at all.

bibliomancy—this is divination using books. pick a book, ask a question, close your eyes, and flip to a random page. with your eyes still closed, point to a random part of the page. open your eyes. that's your answer. sometimes it will be nonsensical or even silly—it's okay to laugh!

cloud gazing—you don't need anything for this except yourself and a cloud-filled sky. find a place to lay on the ground, ask your question, and see which shapes the clouds take on. what do these symbols mean to you, and more importantly, how can they answer your question? let your imagination and intuition run wild!

shufflemancy—i saved the best for last, because in my opinion, this one is the most fun! this is divination using music. all you have to do is get a playlist ready, ask a question, then press shuffle. see which song plays and listen carefully to the lyrics. the answer might surprise you or even move you.

MAGICAL JOURNAL PROMPT: *try at least two of these divination methods (or all three, but only if you're feeling adventurous) and write about how it went. next, think about things you do or use in your daily life—is there a way you can turn some of them into divination? if so, try it out and report back with your findings!*

> more divination methods you can look into as you grow your practice: numerology, norse runes (aka the elder futhark), celtic ogham, tasseography (aka tea leaf reading), palmistry (aka palm reading), and scrying (aka reading a crystal ball or other reflective surface).

she sees a rainbow.

you see a promise of blessings to come.

they see a white feather.

you see a reminder to keep having hope.

he sees a snake.

you see the potential for self-transformation.

—it's all about changing your perspective.

intuition game

divination isn't the only thing that can help you get in touch with your intuition. intuition games like this can exercise the accuracy of your hunches. plus, they're a lot of fun!

WHAT YOU'LL NEED
scrap paper
a writing utensil
a medium to large jar with a lid

DIRECTIONS

begin by taking your scrap paper and tearing it into ten semi-equal pieces. on those pieces, draw any symbols you'd like. some suggestions to get you started are a moon, a star, a sun, a flower, and a butterfly.

fold those pieces of paper in half, and then in half again. toss them into your jar. put the lid on. shake, shake, shake.

next, take the lid off, then reach in and pick a random piece—don't open it right away, though! first, use your intuition to try to guess which symbol is on the paper, and *then* open it. this is a game, after all, so keep track of how many times you get it right!

> pay attention to how it felt when you made the right guess—before you opened the paper and found out for certain. chances are, that's how your intuition will feel when you're right about something in everyday life, which will make trusting yourself in those moments a whole lot easier!

#intuitivestruggles

truthfully, i've only just scratched the surface on working with your intuition. most of that information can't be contained in one book, let alone one section of one book.

that's because your intuition is yours and yours alone; it won't be like anyone else's.

the only way you can learn more about it is to keep paying attention to it and keep exercising it in every way imaginable, and i don't just mean with things like divination or intuition games. anytime you aren't sure what to do—even with small, seemingly inconsequential quandaries like what color you should paint your nails or what show you should binge on netflix—close your eyes and ask your intuition what you should do.

there's always a reason for it, even if you can't see it just yet.

in some ways, listening to your intuition is very easy and natural, because all you're doing is listening to yourself, and that's someone you already know pretty well.

i find it's when you start to clue *other* people into your hunches that you might start to experience some self-doubt.

there have been so many times i've told people about my hunches— like meeting someone who immediately gives me shivers-down-my-spine bad vibes, even though they seem kind and nice on the surface—only to immediately be written off as judgy. even when i'm eventually proven right, it's usually followed up with, "oh, hm. what a coincidence!"

but there are no coincidences with intuition.

promise me you'll never write yourself off just because other people do. you are *not* being overdramatic or delusional for sensing what others won't allow themselves to. if you need to hear it, then here: *i believe you.* but that's not what matters. what matters is that you believe yourself regardless of the pushback.

ignore those doubters.

be your own best friend through thick and through thin, witch.

---

want to learn more about getting in touch with your own unique intuition? i highly recommend picking up one of my favorite books, *the secret psychic* by angela a. wix.

fuck being the same.

every time you see me,
i'll be a different person,
but that doesn't mean
i'm faking anything.

i'm just leaving a welcome mat out
for every version of myself.

i'm entertaining the beauty
of my own comings & goings—
no matter how permanent,
no matter how temporary.

i've never felt more real in my life.

—*you should try it sometime.*

part iii

~~~~~~

your cycles

"cycles?"

yes, cycles!

by definition, cycles are things that happen again and again and again with a definitive beginning and end. there are *so* many cycles you experience on the regular that you might not even be consciously aware of.

whether that means the weekly cycle, the moon cycle, or the seasonal holiday cycle, every one of these cycles has a magical energy that affects us and the world around us.

in this section, i'll be teaching you how you can live your life *and* work your magic going by some of those cycles present in your life.

in my opinion, i think it's always best to work *with* that existing energy instead of trying to work *against* it.

make no mistake, though—you can make whatever kind of magic you want to make whenever you want to make it! you know how i feel about rules in witchcraft: generally speaking, do whatever the hex you want. your witchy intuition should always come first.

however, i *do* find that certain magical acts are more powerful during certain days, moon cycles, and seasonal holidays.

i would venture to say that most experienced witches do, too, even if we don't always agree on what's most powerful and when. (these are, as always, my own takes, based on my own personal experiences as a witch.)

when it comes down to it, why *not* take advantage of these cycles whenever you possibly can?

---

you'll notice that there's a combination of magical journal prompts as well as card pulls/spreads in this section. this is to help keep you in the habit of self-reflecting and working with your intuition.

---

the weekly cycle

let's start with your day-to-day.

each day of the week is associated with a celestial body—mostly planets, as well as the sun and the moon—which gives it an overall energy that is favorable to certain spellwork and other magical doings:

sunday (*the sun*)—this day is often associated with rest in our society, but it's actually a great day to do workings that speak to your power and success. there's a lot of happy energy on this day, too, so let loose and do whatever brings a smile to your face. nurture your inner child.

monday (*the moon*)—usually recognized as the beginning of the work/ school week and therefore the go-get-'em day, nonmagically speaking; magically, it's best to take it slow and tap into your intuition. meditation, divination, and dream-related workings are best performed on this day.

tuesday (*mars*)—this is a much more intense weekday. there's a "fired up" energy that comes along with it, so do workings that require or relate to empowerment, bravery, and strength. follow your passion and confidently create something you love.

wednesday (*mercury*)—there's already a lot of weird energy surrounding this day because it's so in-between. it's not at the beginning of the week, but it's not at the end of the week, either. do something unexpected and outside of the box. express yourself and your magic in new ways.

thursday (*jupiter*)—prosperity and abundance are the themes of this day, and therefore money/career spells are highly encouraged. you may also want to take this time to recognize your self-worth. strive for the things you know you deserve and believe you can achieve them.

friday (*venus*)—it's all about self-love on this day, so take extra special care of yourself and do nonstressful spells that honor *you*. it's also a day for beauty and friendship, so why not get dressed up and spend some time with the people you care about the most?

saturday (*saturn*)—the first day of the weekend is typically considered a time for play and even a bit of partying. magically, it's a day more suited to buckling down and getting super-serious. set boundaries— magical or otherwise—and do some shadow work.

MAGICAL JOURNAL PROMPT: *overall, which day of the week is your favorite and why? once you write down your answer, find that day on my list. does anything surprise you when you compare your reason(s) to the magical significance of that day?*

as you align your magic with the days of the week, you'll find what
works for you. if your intuition tells you to cast a prosperity spell on a
tuesday afternoon, even though thursdays are considered best for that,
go ahead and do it anyway. maybe there's something about tuesday's
energy that works better for *you.*

you may not be inspired to
cast a spell each day,
& this is your
permission not to.

remember:
you. are. the. magic.

therefore, you infuse
stardust into
every single thing
your fingers touch.

—how amazing is that?

sunday

nurturing your inner child

we all have an inner child: a version of yourself that just wants to play, giggle, and make backyard mudpies—those were always fun, weren't they?

sadly, as we become adults, that side becomes less and less accepted by society. if we do the things we did freely back when we were kids, we get called *immature* or *childish*. we often begin to believe that we should only be engaging in serious things like work, doctor's appointments, and taxes, so we suppress our inner child and forget to nurture that side of ourselves altogether.

it's important that you try to break free from these restrictions—not just on sunday, whose joyous energy particularly speaks to your inner child, but every day.

because i was raised in an unstable home, i had to grow up very fast— faster than i should have had to. i feel like i didn't get to fully enjoy the things kids were supposed to because i was too busy trying to cope with big, difficult things i barely understood.

for me, part of nurturing my inner child means letting myself do the things i missed out on, like reading middle grade books that remind me of the world's magic or playing games that affirm that it's okay to have fun.

it's so much more than that, though. my feelings were often ignored as a child, so i find i have trouble being vulnerable with other people as an adult. the idea of crying in front of someone—even someone i trust— almost causes me physical pain. to nurture my inner child, i constantly have to make sure to stop and remind myself that my feelings are valid and nothing bad is going to happen to me for showing them.

there are so many ways to nurture your inner child, depending on what you've experienced. start by giving your adult self the love your child self never received.

MAGICAL JOURNAL PROMPT: *what are a few things that you loved to do when you were a child? why don't you do them today? is it because you genuinely grew out of them, or is it because you don't think you're supposed to do them anymore?*

* * **CARD PULL** * *

what is one
thing i can do
to nurture my
inner child
right now?

sunday
spell for success

what better way to begin your week than with an easy, breezy spell that sets you up for success?

WHAT YOU'LL NEED
a piece of scrap paper
a writing utensil
the sun

DIRECTIONS

on your piece of scrap paper, write down one thing you want to achieve this week, making sure to word it as an affirmation: "this week, i am super-successful at _____."

it can be a specific goal you have—like starting or finishing a creative project—or something simple like "finding joy in the little things."

afterward, leave this piece of scrap paper on a windowsill the sun reaches or somewhere outside in direct sunlight. remember to repeat your affirmation as you set it down, followed by, "so mote it be."

that's pretty much it!

feel free to leave it there until the sun goes down.

you see, the sun—which sunday is named after—is already known for energizing things, and it can certainly energize your goals, too.

if it's cloudy outside, no worries. the sun is too powerful to be totally cast out; it's always somewhere just beyond the clouds. your spell will still work fine. alternatively, you could also place your affirmation underneath the sun tarot card or a citrine crystal (associated with sun energy), and that would work just as well. it's all about that symbolism, witch.

* * CARD SPREAD * *

CARD 1	CARD 2	CARD 3
what is my idea of success?	what kind of success is realistic for me this week?	which path can i take to get there?

monday

practicing meditation

in my nonexpert opinion, meditation is one of the most important things you can do for your overall well-being, as it has the power to reduce stress, balance moods, and promote peaceful sleep. (because i've always struggled to sleep, it's been life-changing for me.)

many of us have also found that going within and finding stillness can help you discern the voice of your intuition as well.

there are just too many benefits to *not* do it.

if you haven't meditated before, you might think it's just sitting down, closing your eyes, and wiping your mind free of thoughts—it's no wonder that sounds boring and even impossible to most people. while that's sort of a type of meditation, it's far from the only one.

anything that brings you into present awareness can be meditation; for that reason, it's also a great grounding technique.

i do a three- or five-minute meditation every morning. that's all you really need—just a few spare minutes. you don't even have to meditate every single day if you don't want to. add it to your monday routine at first and see what it brings to your life as well as your magical journey.

a typical meditation would be to go to a quiet place, sit comfortably, set an alarm for your desired amount of time, and close your eyes (or at least soften your focus) until your alarm goes off. during your meditation, try not to spend too much energy fighting your thoughts—just accept that they're going to happen and pay them as little mind as possible (some days will be easier than others). let go and just *be* for a few minutes.

if this doesn't work for you, however, there are countless other ways to meditate:

take a walk—as much as it might pain you, do this *without* headphones. concentrate instead on the sounds of nature, people, and life. let all judgments fall away. simply be aware. see what you notice. (this might be hard to achieve the first few times; just do your best.)

look at a tarot/oracle card—pick your favorite card and display it at eye level. gaze upon it and try not to fixate too much on any one detail as you consider what it means. you can play soft instrumental music in the background to help you relax.

work with water—monday is associated with the moon, which is associated with water because it tugs at the tides. it can be very calming to meditate with. find a body of water like a lake, a river, or an ocean and focus your attention on it. raindrops also work. if none of this is doable, you can fill something like a bathtub, bowl, or cup. when all else fails, pull up a water-centric video on youtube!

* ✳ CARD SPREAD ✳ *

CARD 1	*CARD 2*
how will i benefit from meditation?	what is the best form of meditation for me?

monday
spell bag for serene dreams

my spouse wasn't always a huge believer in magic, but even before they were, they noticed that they got better rest when i made them one of these. (this is *not* a replacement for medical care regarding serious issues, though.) it's also great if you want to increase the intuitive messages you receive in your dreams.

WHAT YOU'LL NEED
a small drawstring pouch
dried lavender buds
dried rosebuds/rose petals (for beauty rest *. . . get it?)*
amethyst crystal chips

DIRECTIONS

spell bags are my favorite because they're like crockpot recipes—just throw the spell ingredients into the bag and let it work its magic!

103

as you add each ingredient to your bag, remember to say a positive affirmation, like, "i sleep soundly every single night. my intuition speaks to me loud and clear through my dreams. i always wake up feeling well-rested." you get the gist. tailor it however you need to.

when you're done, say "so mote it be," and then go place it underneath your pillow or tuck it inside of your pillowcase. (i highly recommend the latter in case it breaks open while you're fast asleep, which actually happened to me during the very week i was writing this chapter. needless to say, tucking it into my pillowcase saved me from a huge mess!)

make sure you cleanse your spell bag every monday to keep its energy fresh. if i forget to do this, i find that my sleep becomes more restless, or i may see an increase in nightmares.

MAGICAL JOURNAL PROMPT: *whenever you have a dream, make it a habit to write it down. even the silliest and most nonsensical dreams can have an underlying intuitive message that can be useful for your waking life. what happened from beginning to end? was anyone else in your dream, and did they say anything? what symbolism did you notice, if any, and what does it mean to you?*

* ✳ CARD SPREAD ✳ *

CARD 1	CARD 2	CARD 3
a card to represent the theme of last night's dream.	what lesson or message can i take away from the dream?	how can i apply this lesson/message to my life?

tuesday

reigniting your passion

between passing long, exhausting hours at work or school, spending time with family and friends, and (perhaps) organizing side hustles for basic survival in this capitalist hellscape, who has the time or energy to find something to be *passionate* about?

not many.

the idea of carving time out for yourself might not only seem impossible or impractical, but it might even give you feelings of guilt. i, too, have had thoughts like, "but i could be giving my time to someone else!" and "i could be doing something productive instead."

i'm sorry, but *fuck* being productive.

most of us are productive all day long.

take the time to find something you're passionate about and do it, even if it's just for an hour or so every tuesday, because life is so much more than just working and making money. that's not to say those things aren't necessary (anyone who says otherwise is probably incredibly privileged and needs a major reality check), but you're worthy of having so much *more*.

while you're at it, i ask you to consider *not* turning everything you're passionate about into a side hustle or career.

when i was a little girl, i spent a lot of my time playing computer games as a much-needed escape from my painful reality. though i've done a lot of healing, i still play those games today; they give me a lot of comfort.

i've had people ask me why i don't become a gaming streamer. the truth is, i want games to be the one thing that remains sacred to me, the one thing i do that's just for my enjoyment and no one else's. i don't want it to become a stressor or an obligation. i deserve that one thing, and so do you. your passion is part of your magic, even if you don't share it with anyone else. it's magic for no other reason than it lights you up.

MAGICAL JOURNAL PROMPT: *what's your passion? if you're not sure, what do you think it could be? maybe it's something you've always liked but haven't had a chance to dive into, something i've mentioned somewhere in this book, like tarot or crystals, or something interesting someone mentioned to you in passing. go ahead and see that curiosity through.*

* ✳ CARD SPREAD ✳ *

CARD 1	CARD 2
what does it look like when i follow my passion?	what does it look like when i don't?

tuesday

spell to spark change

i live in a country where, at the time i'm writing this, rights to abortion care are being stripped away, guns are favored over human lives, and books written by and/or about marginalized people are being banned. this is unacceptable. may this spell light a fire in you to spark fierce change in our world.

WHAT YOU'LL NEED

your magical journal

a writing utensil

your phone

powdered cinnamon

an orange candle in a holder

a lighter or match

DIRECTIONS

first, you'll have to pick a political or societal topic you're passionate about, such as one of those i listed above. (you may want to pick something that's fresh and relevant at the exact time you're reading this.) what change is it that you would like to see?

take a page out of your magical journal and write it at the top, followed by an affirmation: "i am able to help make this change happen. i put in all of the necessary work. i do not give up until i see justice."

next, you're going to write up your own game plan—a list of things you can personally do to make this change.

this can mean voting, protesting, signing petitions, making donations, or something else entirely. nothing—as long as it's *something*—is too little to make a difference. depending on the issue, you may need to do some research to see which course of action would be best, which can also be part of doing the work.

first, take a picture of your list so you have a clean version to refer to later. now sprinkle a tiny pinch of cinnamon on the paper to give yourself the energy needed to go through with this plan. fold the paper in half twice (keeping the cinnamon inside) and place your orange candle on top of it. as you light it, don't forget to say, "so mote it be."

* ✳ CARD PULL ✳ *

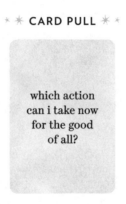

which action
can i take now
for the good
of all?

wednesday
using your voice

if you've read my poetry, then you know i often write about the painful things i've gone through: child abuse, eating disorders, toxic relationships, and more.

to some, i make writing about those things look easy and effortless.

it has been anything but.

when i self-published my first poetry collection, *the princess saves herself in this one*, i initially kept it a secret from everyone in my life. (well, *almost* everyone, with the exception of my now-spouse and a few of my closest friends, who have been there for me every step of the way.)

princess was the story of my life up until that point, and i shared a lot of previously unspoken truths on those pages, especially when it came to the mistreatment i had endured at the hands of my deceased mother.

i was afraid if my loved ones found out about my book and read it, they would invalidate my trauma or even be angry with me. at worst, i imagined that they would abandon me.

eventually, i decided that i didn't want to keep my book a secret anymore. i was very proud of it, and i wanted to share it with everyone in my life. to my surprise, most of my loved ones supported me; however, it was made clear to me that a few people did not. so many of my fears came true, and it was hard to cope with for a while.

despite that, if i were given the opportunity to do it all over, i wouldn't change a thing. i spent too much of my life suffering in silence in order to keep the peace. speaking up helped me heal, and from what others have told me, it helped them heal, too.

wednesday is the day of communication. to recognize your magic is to recognize the power of your words, so when someone hurts you, let them know. when someone interrupts you, keep talking until you say everything you need to say. most importantly, tell your story with honesty and inspire others to do the same.

if you need some assistance, light a blue candle, carry an aquamarine crystal, or display the queen of swords tarot card on your altar.

MAGICAL JOURNAL PROMPT: *what's one truth you've been keeping inside? why? what's the worst thing that could happen if you spoke it aloud? what's the best thing?*

* * CARD SPREAD * *

CARD 1	CARD 2	CARD 3
my filtered self.	my unfiltered self.	how do i balance them?

wednesday

spell to push you out of your comfort zone

people are often afraid of switching things up and doing something a little different, even if they want to. that's because it can mean taking a risk, like looking silly or embarrassing themselves. but if you don't take a chance and do it, how will you ever know? even if it doesn't go the way you wanted, at least you'll figure out whether or not it's for you. go ahead and cast this spell to help push you out of your comfort zone!

WHAT YOU'LL NEED
your magical journal
scrap paper
a writing utensil
a small to medium bowl
a rainbow moonstone crystal

DIRECTIONS

MAGICAL JOURNAL PROMPT: *write a list of five to ten things you can do to switch things up. think of things you want to do but have been putting off out of fear. perhaps it's something small and subtle like "wearing my hair in a new style" or big and scary like "asking someone out for coffee" (platonically or romantically).*

do the magical journal exercise. then prepare as many pieces of scrap paper as you need. write down each point from your list, each on its own paper. when you're done, fold each piece of paper in half twice.

next, take all your folded pieces of paper and deposit them in the bowl. create a hollow space in the middle of the bowl and place the rainbow moonstone crystal there.

pick a paper out of the bowl. commit to doing whatever it tells you to do by turning it into an affirmation: "today, i welcome the new experience of _____ and everything that it has to teach me. so mote it be." carry the crystal with you so it can energetically support you. cleanse it and return it to your bowl when you're done. pull out a new piece of paper every wednesday. the more chances you take, the easier it'll become!

✳ CARD SPREAD ✳

CARD 1	CARD 2	CARD 3
a card to describe my comfort zone.	what am i currently losing out on by staying inside of it?	how to break free.

MAKE YOUR OWN MAGIC

thursday
knowing your worth

on top of the abuse and neglect i endured at home as a child, many of the
people around me—such as my peers and even some authority figures—
made it clear that my thoughts, feelings, and well-being were not of any
importance. eventually, i began to believe i wasn't all that important,
either, which later manifested as:

- surrounding myself with people who didn't value me nearly as much as
  i valued them.

- being afraid to add to conversations because i didn't think anyone
  cared about my opinions or perspectives.

- staying with partners who constantly put me down and kept me second
  to others.

- not saying anything when my needs weren't being met because i didn't
  want to be an inconvenience.

- feeling uncomfortable and even ashamed when someone gave me a
  gift, or whenever the spotlight was put on me.

these are all things i still struggle with. the difference is, i now have the
awareness to recognize these issues and work on healing them.

i know i'm not the only one who struggles with self-worth—maybe you
do, too. if so, then this is your reminder that just because other people
have failed to *see* your importance doesn't mean that you aren't important.

you *are* important, so start acting like it, witch.

no matter who you may be, and no matter what may have happened
to you in the past, you very much still deserve to have and experience

wonderful things. pay close attention to this on thursdays, and don't you dare settle for less than what you know you deserve—not from others, and certainly not from yourself.

MAGICAL JOURNAL PROMPT: *describe a time when someone didn't see your value. did this experience affect you in the long term? how? now describe a time when you didn't see your own value and how that continues to impact you. are these two instances connected in any way?*

✷ CARD SPREAD ✷

CARD 1	*CARD 2*
what i think i'm worthy of.	what i'm actually worthy of.

thursday
spell jar for prosperity

some witches don't believe in doing spells for money or material gain, but i disagree. in my opinion, there's no shame in using your magic to make sure you're taken care of in every way. you need money to survive, after all. this spell jar is to help you attract more prosperity into your life.

WHAT YOU'LL NEED
a medium jar with a lid
dried peppermint leaves
dried chamomile flowers
a citrine crystal
three coins of your choice

DIRECTIONS

fill your jar with your dried peppermint leaves and dried chamomile flowers, making sure to leave plenty of empty space at the top—this is the "base" of your spell jar, so to speak.

next, arrange your citrine crystal and three coins on top of your herb base. when you're pleased with how it looks, put the lid on your jar.

hold the jar in your hands and say this affirmation: "prosperity is growing and flourishing in my life. i am abundant in all things amazing. i am worthy of all the blessings being bestowed upon me. so mote it be."

keep your spell jar on your altar however long you'd like. i like to keep one there permanently, refreshing the herbs every few weeks or months, usually on a thursday.

it's important to know that your spell jar alone won't get you money. you'll need to actively put yourself in situations to increase your chances of receiving it, so apply for jobs, request a promotion, and ask for donations—stuff like that. as you do, you may find that you attract more. be on the lookout because you may receive in unexpected ways—including prosperity in forms other than money.

* * CARD PULL * *

which action
can i take to
invite more
prosperity into
my life?

friday
being a better friend to yourself

friday is a day dedicated in part to friendship.

confession: i've never had a lot of friends.

i was a painfully shy child and a very socially awkward and depressed teenager, so it was difficult for me to make them as well as keep them.

i still have visions of myself sitting alone at a long, empty lunch table for years on end. (what i wouldn't give to go back in time and give that child a *huge* hug . . .)

115

eventually, i became so desperate for friends that i clung to the few i *did* have for as long as i possibly could. i did this even if they treated me poorly, because i knew that i would end up completely alone without them.

the very idea terrified me.

i mean, what if i never made a friend again?

so i kept letting people treat me poorly and kept clinging to people who made my life worse instead of better, even in adulthood.

sometimes we're so busy trying to be good friends to other people that we forget that we need to be a good friend to ourselves, too.

part of being a good friend to yourself is letting go of people who are no longer good for you and trusting that better people will come along.

i'll admit that i still have some trouble doing this, especially if that person has been in my life for a long time. it feels like i'm spitting in the face of our happy memories. i completely lose sight of the fact that i can keep those old happy memories while i move on to make new ones elsewhere.

letting go of people doesn't mean that you have to cut them off and shut them out (though that can be necessary at times). sometimes it just means creating a little distance—loving those people from afar, no matter how hard it is, so you can finally focus on and love *yourself* better.

* * CARD SPREAD * *

CARD 1	CARD 2	CARD 3
what does my friendship with myself look like rn?	what would it look like at its healthiest?	one small step i can take toward that.

friday
spell for magical self-love

acts of self-love are healing for the heart. *magical* acts of self-love take that one step further.

WHAT YOU'LL NEED
pink himalayan salt
a small bowl
a rose quartz crystal
a pink amethyst crystal
a rose water face mask (optional)
your magical journal
a writing utensil

DIRECTIONS

first things first: pour pink himalayan salt into a small bowl to gently cleanse away any energy that's not aligned with self-love and place it somewhere on your altar.

now, to invite in energy that *is* aligned with self-love, place a rose quartz crystal beside the bowl on one side and a pink amethyst crystal on the other. (you can just use two rose quartz crystals or one rose quartz + one purple amethyst crystal if you don't have pink amethyst, which is a little harder to come by.)

if you have a rose water face mask, apply it as directed. remember to remove it whenever the package recommends.

next, get out your magical journal and follow this prompt:

MAGICAL JOURNAL PROMPT: *list at least three things that you love about yourself, but if you can keep going, then definitely do so. this can include your physical appearance, but don't stop there. there is so much more to you, like your personality, accomplishments, and skills. perhaps you love your brown eyes, how empathetic you are, or the way you never give up in the face of adversity.*

if you're having trouble thinking of things to add to your list, try the card spread below.

* ✳ CARD SPREAD ✳ *

CARD 1	CARD 2	CARD 3
one reason to love myself.	a second reason.	a third reason.

once you're finished with your list, i want you to tenderly place your hand over your heart while you read this list aloud, signing off with, as always, "so mote it be." challenge: try to list new things you love about yourself during each magical friday self-love session!

saturday

doing shadow work

shadow work is a phrase you'll see a lot of in witchcraft spaces . . . but what does that term actually *mean*?

for me, it's about going within and facing the things i keep hidden in my shadows—painful memories, past mistakes, truths that bring me feelings of shame. these things can be easier to ignore than to deal with, so i hide them not just from others but from myself.

shadow work is about bringing those things into the light so that i can work through them and/or integrate them into my "everyday" self.

i dissect painful memories to see how i'm allowing them to negatively impact all areas of my life.

i own up to my mistakes and appreciate how they've helped me become the person i am today.

i face the truth of who i am, even if it's not always pretty, even if it makes me less "perfect" to myself and/or others.

but that's just the beginning—to do the actual *act* of shadow work, i create a safe and protected space for myself, pick a topic, and journal my every thought. i like to think that i'm writing my way through acceptance and healing.

here's how:

MAGICAL JOURNAL PROMPT: *try* freewriting *to do your saturday shadow* *work.* which shadows have been following you? *pick up your pen and spill* *your thoughts on the page for ten to fifteen minutes (be sure to set a timer)—* *you'd be surprised how much you have to say!*

you can use your tarot/oracle cards as a guide through your shadow work, too:

✶ ✷ CARD SPREAD ✷ ✶

CARD 1

something about myself that i hide out of fear or shame.

CARD 2

why i hide it.

CARD 3

what good would come from accepting this part of myself?

asking yourself these questions may bring up some tough emotions. if you feel overwhelmed, please don't hesitate to call a trusted friend or family member or seek professional guidance in whatever way it's available to you.

saturday
spell to strengthen your boundaries

i don't know about you, but i give away so much of my energy to others, like agreeing to conversations, activities, or favors i don't have the bandwidth for. this can happen with friends, family, peers, bosses, coworkers—*anyone*. sometimes we just want to make sure the people in our lives are happy and taken care of, even if it drains us and makes *us* unhappy. that's never okay. this spell can help you strengthen your boundaries before the new week.

WHAT YOU'LL NEED
4 black candles in holders
a lighter or match

DIRECTIONS

sit on the floor in front of your altar and place the four black candles on the floor in the space surrounding your body: one in front of you, one to your left, one to your right, and one behind you. (this effectively creates a protective boundary around you. make sure you give yourself plenty of space in case you want to stretch out and stay for a while.)

as you light each candle, repeat these affirmations:

◆ "i am no longer willing to give more of myself than i want to or am able to."

◆ "i only say yes to the things i want to do."

◆ "i allow myself to say no to things that don't excite me without feelings of guilt."

◆ "these boundaries are nonnegotiable, and i stop at nothing to make sure they're respected by myself and others."

stay in this space and contemplate your boundaries as the candles burn. when the candles have burned all the way down or you're ready to be done, say "so mote it be." you *might* want to do this spell every saturday to help you recover from a long week of giving your energy away. if you extinguished your candles before they burned completely, feel free to use them next time.

✶ ✶ CARD SPREAD ✶ ✶

CARD 1	*CARD 2*	*CARD 3*
where am i currently lacking boundaries?	how might this harm me?	the push i need to assert my boundaries.

the moon cycle

the moon cycle lasts approximately thirty days from beginning to end. during this time, you may find that the magical energy around you and within you shifts and changes as well. (after all, the moon controls the tides and we know from science class that we're mostly made up of water, so it makes total sense that it would affect us so much.)

while there are technically eight moon phases total because the waxing and waning phases are split into several smaller stages, we're going to stick with the four main phases to keep it nice and simple for now. (why make shit more complicated than it needs to be?)

go ahead and look up the dates of the phases in the coming days. mark them in your calendar and try making magic with the moon, beginning with the new moon and going through the waning moon, if possible. see what works for you and tweak what doesn't.

new moon—this is the first phase of the moon cycle. when the moon becomes completely dark, it brings the energy of a fresh slate and new beginnings into every area of your life. manifestation spells and rituals are *very* commonly performed during this phase.

waxing moon—after manifesting during the new moon, it's time to put in the work alongside our waxing friend. as the moon grows in size, prepare to get busy and take action toward your goals so they can come into fruition during the full moon.

full moon—celebrate your accomplishments! full moon = full power, so do any spell you'd like. this is also an excellent time for releasing rituals; as the moon comes full circle, so do many things in your life, so say farewell to anything you don't need anymore.

waning moon—as the moon wanes—or begins to disappear—you should wane, too. i'm *not* saying that you should literally disappear (you shouldn't), but you may want to take a breather from all the work and celebrating you did during the waxing and full moon phases. self-reflect and show gratitude for the journey you just had before a new cycle starts.

MAGICAL JOURNAL PROMPT: *tonight, go outside or to a window and gaze up at the moon. silently take note of the phase as well as how you're feeling, not just physically but emotionally. do you think this could possibly be correlated to the moon phase? why or why not?*

when she's all aglow,
she's all anyone can talk about.

when she retreats into the shadows,
she's *still* all anyone can talk about.

—*i want to be more like the moon.*

new moon

starting over

it's never too late to start over.

you don't have to stay at the job you hate or keep working toward a degree that no longer sparks passion in you.

you don't have to maintain relationships that don't make sense for you anymore.

you don't have to keep reading the same kind of books, listening to the same kind of music, or eating the same kind of food.

you don't have to adhere to the same beliefs or values you've always had.

you don't have to keep waking up and doing all of the things that no longer make you the happiest version of yourself.

we can get stuck in our ways when we're used to doing and being certain things, but the truth is that you don't have to be the same person you were yesterday. you can just decide to be different one day—to follow a new routine, to have new goals, to go in an unexpected direction.

and you don't need anyone's permission to do so, except for your own.

that's not to say that starting over will be easy. in many ways, it won't be. there were times i've decided to enact major changes to make my life more authentically mine, only to be met with negative reactions from the people around me.

for example, when i decided to call myself a witch, i did lose a friend or two who clearly disapproved (though they would never admit it).

people don't like change, but they *especially* don't like it when the people close to them start to change. perhaps it's because they feel like they're being judged for their own personal choices (even though they aren't), or perhaps it's because they aren't growing as much as they'd like and they don't like being reminded of that.

the new moon gives you an exciting blank slate to work with, so make the most of it and ignore anyone who wants less for you.

perhaps you should take this time to connect with people who are more aligned with who you are now and who you want to become.

* ✳ CARD PULL ✳ *

what new
beginning awaits
me this
moon cycle?

new moon
manifestation

to manifest is to magic up your desires, to make them a reality. that's what you've done for all of your spells so far, but new moon manifestation spells and rituals are special because you can magic up a whole list of things that don't necessarily have to do with one another—almost like your own magical wish list!

WHAT YOU'LL NEED
your magical journal
a writing utensil
bay leaves
a sharpie
a cauldron or firesafe dish
a long lighter or match

DIRECTIONS

first, start by *thinking* of things you would like to manifest. this isn't something that should be rushed, so you might want to take a few days to really ponder it. ask yourself, *what does my ideal life look like?* then go from there. try not to set limits on yourself.

MAGICAL JOURNAL PROMPT: *at the top of the page, write, "for the good of all and with harm to none, i manifest the following things or better." next, write your list of manifestations as if they're already true. get specific and include how they make you feel. for example, "i'm so excited now that i'm a successful small business owner/social media influencer." write "so mote it be" at the bottom of the page to finalize it.*

get your bay leaves and sharpie. on each bay leaf, write one of your manifestations. (you can write a few keywords if they're too long to fit— that's what i do!)

start to transfer the bay leaves into your cauldron. take your lighter/match and carefully burn each one, which will send your manifestations out into the world via fire energy. (using a long lighter/match is important because bay leaf flames tend to get large quick.)

the next morning, dispose of the ashes however you wish. some witches like to save them and mix them with table salt to make their own black salt for future spellwork.

* ✳ CARD SPREAD ✳ *

CARD 1	CARD 2	CARD 3
what i think i'm capable of manifesting.	what i'm actually capable of manifesting.	how to rise to the challenge of surpassing my own expectations.

new moon

when your manifestations don't come true

oh no—you manifested something, but it's been a while and nothing's happened!

this is a scenario every witch has experienced.

here are a few things to consider:

give it a moment—not all magic is instantaneous. some things take time. did you allow the proper space for your manifestation to happen, or are you being impatient? if you can, try to take your mind off it. remember the phrase "a watched pot never boils"? obsessing over it won't help your case!

you may not be ready yet—this might be frustrating to hear, but i know from experience this may be the case. years ago, i tried manifesting a publishing deal for a tarot deck, but my proposed tarot deck project turned into an oracle deck instead. though i loved cocreating my oracle deck, the idea of cocreating a tarot deck never left my mind. a few years later, after becoming more familiar with tarot and taking a few courses on it, i finally received the opportunity to publish my own tarot deck. i ended up cocreating the deck of my dreams. looking back, i'm glad i didn't get to make a tarot deck when i first wanted to. i wasn't ready yet, and if i had tried before i was truly ready, it wouldn't have been the best it could have been. my manifestation found me when it was time.

it actually did manifest—sometimes our manifestations come true and we don't even realize it because there's a disconnect between our expectations and reality. you might be disappointed by the *way* it came true, but that doesn't mean it *didn't* come true. try again the next new moon and be more specific with what you manifest and how it makes you feel.

something better is brewing—maybe you didn't dream big enough (that's why you should never sell yourself short), or maybe the dream you had isn't the best thing for you when it comes down to it. be open to the possibilities—you might be in for some amazing surprises!

there might be real-world barriers—i would be remiss not to mention
that systems of oppression such as racism, sexism, classism,
homophobia, and fatphobia are built to keep some people
down while building others up. these things could affect your
manifestations/spellwork. it can be exhausting to deal with these
obstacles, but try to keep your chin up and don't be too hard on
yourself. you are *not* a weak witch; society is a seriously fucked-up
place in need of significant change.

waxing moon
making moves

all my life i've been an avid reader.

eventually i started to have dreams about being a writer myself.

i wrote a few poems here and there and even the occasional short
story. i wanted so badly to write a full-length book of my own, but i wasn't
very consistent with it. it usually began with a burst of inspiration and
sometimes a few written pages before it fizzled out.

my follow-through? pretty bad.

if only i had opened my eyes and realized that my dreams wouldn't
become reality unless i actually did something about them.

here's the thing.

if you want your manifestations/spells to come true, your efforts can't
stop after you say, "so mote it be." in my experience, things *will* sometimes
drop into your lap, but most of the time, the magic will happen because
you continue to speak words and take actions that align with your desires,
especially during the waxing moon.

i know that i never would have become an author if i didn't stop telling myself, "i can't do this" or "it's too difficult," if i didn't push myself to put pen to paper and keep going until i scribbled the words "the end."

i find that we procrastinate about the things that are important to us because we're afraid of getting them wrong. it's okay to be afraid, but take that fear and use it as fuel to lead you through it. maybe it'll be a disaster, or maybe it'll be wonderful. you won't find out 'til you try, will you?

"if i have to do so much work, what's the point of casting spells?" some of you might be asking.

think of it like this: the spell gives you a metaphorical set of wings. it's up to you whether or not you actually take flight.

MAGICAL JOURNAL PROMPT: *when it comes to your current dreams and goals, what are you most afraid of getting wrong?*

* ✳ CARD SPREAD ✳ *

CARD 1	CARD 2
what am i procrastinating about?	how would i feel if i finally stopped making excuses and got it done?

waxing moon
spell for motivation

you may not always feel like putting in work toward your manifestations, even during the waxing moon. i totally get it. whether you need to start a new task, continue one, or finish one, it can be intimidating. cast this quick little spell whenever you need to get motivated to check something off your to-do list.

WHAT YOU'LL NEED
a piece of scrap paper
a writing utensil
a small bowl
coffee beans

DIRECTIONS

on your piece of scrap paper, write down the immediate goal that you need motivation to smash.

next, go ahead and place your bowl on your altar. alternatively, you may also use a lid to a jar, or even a condiment bowl, if you happen to have one on hand.

pour your coffee beans (alternatively, you can use coffee grounds) inside of the bowl, filling it up about halfway. you know how we drink coffee for energy and motivation in the morning? we can use it in our spells for the same thing!

on top of your bed of coffee beans, place your piece of scrap paper. as you sprinkle a few more coffee beans on top of the paper, repeat the following affirmation: "i am motivated to complete this goal of _____. i know how to get shit done. nothing and no one can stop me, including myself. so mote it be."

all done!

this spell is only designed for one goal at a time, but you can do it as often as you wish—even multiple times a day with different goals. the best part is that it will likely only take a few minutes of your time.

⋆ ✳ CARD SPREAD ✳ ⋆

CARD 1	CARD 2	CARD 3
one small and impressive thing i can achieve today.	one big and impressive thing i can achieve today.	a card to give me the push i need.

full moon
celebrating yourself

i'm the kind of person who achieves something and then wants to move on to the next sparkly thing almost immediately.

even as i write this book, i'm already thinking about which book i'm going to write next—what the title will be, what the cover will look like, how i'm going to format the contents inside . . .

you should always take time to pause and celebrate your achievements, no matter how big or small. don't blow past anything as though it's insignificant. if you do, you're going to feel empty later on when you look back and realize that you once dreamed of being exactly where you are now, yet you didn't stop to appreciate the journey it took to get there.

(i'm trying to be better about doing this, i swear!)

no, you don't have to throw an entire party with a long guest list every time you get an A+ on a paper, nail down your dream client, or have one of your manifestations come true. it doesn't have to be that dramatic.

celebrating can mean *so* many different things.

celebrating can mean eating dinner alone outside so you can watch the sunset.

celebrating can mean going down to your favorite bakery and getting a little treat for yourself. (i may or may not have done this yesterday.)

celebrating can mean stopping to give yourself a silent but heartfelt "congratulations."

when witches talk about full moon rituals, they're usually talking about releasing rituals. however, i think we should also normalize self-celebration as a ritual, even if it doesn't involve a spell. celebrate what deserves celebrating, *then* get rid of what no longer serves.

* * CARD PULL * *

what have i
achieved this
moon cycle that
deserves to be
acknowledged?

full moon
releasing

yay, your first full moon releasing spell will soon be underway! get ready to energetically release anything you don't want to bring with you into the next moon cycle. this makes room for new manifestations to come your way.

WHAT YOU'LL NEED
your magical journal

a writing utensil

scrap paper

a garbage can

DIRECTIONS

MAGICAL JOURNAL PROMPT: *at the top of the page, write, "for the good of all and with harm to none, i release the following things with love." make your list. for example, "the goals (get specific) that don't suit me anymore," "my self-sabotaging behavior," and "my disappointment over the things that didn't work out." sign off with "so mote it be."*

next, get out your scrap paper and tear it into pieces big enough to write on. on each piece, write down one of the things you'd like to release. keywords work, too.

here comes the fun part.

when you're finished, take those pieces of scrap paper and rip them into teeny tiny bits. as you tear up each one, say, "i hereby release _____ from my life."

where do we throw all the expired things we know longer want?

right into the trash.

yep, trash can be magical, too.

go ahead and throw all those little bits of paper into your nearest garbage can. make sure you take the bag out on trash day so you can get it as far away from your person as possible. you don't need that shit anymore.

cathartic, isn't it?

* * CARD SPREAD * *

CARD 1

what in my life currently belongs in the trash?

CARD 2

what lessons can be salvaged from this before i say goodbye?

CARD 3

how can i make sure it stays gone?

full moon
making moon water

you can make moon water during *any* moon phase, depending on what kind of magic you want to do with it, but the full moon = full power, so it's the most favorable time. whatever intention you give it will be potent.

to make moon water, fill an airtight container with tap water. whisper an affirmation into it, then close it. leave the container under the full moon or in a window, which will magically supercharge it. you can also surround the container with crystals, herbs, or cards that correspond with your intention. just make sure you go out and grab it before the sun comes out!

how to use your moon water:

drink it—sip on it as it is or use it to make tea, coffee, or hot cocoa. as you drink the liquid, you will also drink its magical energy.

cleanse with it—wash your face/hands with it or pour some into a bath to cleanse yourself. you can cleanse your water-safe magical tools with it as well.

bless with it—moon water is basically a witch's holy water, so you can use it to magically bless yourself, your tools, or anything else.

waning moon
getting rest

when you're laser-focused on your goals and manifestations all the time, you can forget to stop and smell the lavender.

you might neglect to nurture your mind, body, and soul altogether by getting less sleep, abandoning any number of your interests and hobbies, or forgoing time with loved ones.

luckily, the waning moon is a nice little pause before the next moon cycle.

during the waning moon, take out your calendar and do some serious reassessing. i bet there's at least *one* thing each week until the new moon that can be put on the back burner or one thing so unnecessarily draining that it can be taken off the calendar altogether.

once you free up some time for yourself, i want you to sit and do nothing, or at least something pleasant that doesn't require too much of your energy. catch up on a tv show that you like or hang out with a low-maintenance friend who's okay with doing something a little more chill and laid-back for the day.

i have this thing where even when i'm supposedly resting, i eventually start thinking about all the things i have to do when my time is up. it can tie my stomach into knots and make me super-anxious. there have been instances where i've even stopped resting so i could begin that work and make those feelings go away.

that is *not* actually resting, and i know i'm far from the only one who has these tendencies.

neglecting to properly recharge between the chapters of your life will inevitably lead to some major burnout, and that's not something you can feasibly work through (at least not well). this could delay your progress instead, so do future-you a major favor and rest during the waning moon so you can go into the next moon cycle more refreshed than ever before!

what can i
do to mentally,
emotionally,
or physically
unwind
right now?

waning moon
spell for gratitude

when was the last time you counted your blessings? some believe that when you show gratitude, you're energetically calling in more things to be grateful for. through the duration of the moon cycle (from the last new moon until now), keep track of all your joyful moments by taking photos and videos on your phone. (tip: make albums to organize them by moon cycle.) they'll be important for this waning moon spell.

WHAT YOU'LL NEED
a silver candle in a holder
a lighter or match
your phone
your magical journal
a writing utensil

DIRECTIONS

light your silver candle and say, "my self-reflection brightens my perspective."

take out your phone and go through your moon cycle photos/videos, but don't flip through them like it's an old, dusty photo album your aunt mildred gave you to look at. pore over each one slowly. take the time to really *remember* what it was like to be in that moment. explore every tiny, microscopic detail—how it felt, how it smelled, how it sounded. shamelessly relive your happiness so you can more effectively write about it.

now do the following journaling.

MAGICAL JOURNAL PROMPT: *write "for all of the following things i am incredibly grateful and i welcome more like them into my life" at the top of the page. use your photos/videos to guide you through making your list, but feel free to include anything else that comes to mind. end with "so mote it be."*

let the candle burn down or extinguish it and use it for your next gratitude spell.

additionally, you can post a photo/video dump to social media so you can show the world how much you have to be grateful for (without being show-offy). not only will this send extra magical energy out there, but it might inspire others to be grateful for their blessings, too.

✧ CARD SPREAD ✧

CARD 1	*CARD 2*
which one of my blessings might i be overlooking?	how can i properly show gratitude for it?

the seasonal holiday cycle

you can work with the magical energy of the seasons by aligning with the seasonal holiday cycle, aka the wheel of the year.

by connecting with the earth in this way, you may find that you're much more in tune with yourself, as the seasons often reflect what's going on in our own lives at the same time.

most of these holidays are on different days every year, so look them up before you mark them down on your calendar. you can even buy a witchy calendar with the dates already incorporated. most will also include the moon phases.

the approximate dates below are for the *northern hemisphere*. (for the southern hemisphere, look to the opposite side of the wheel for the correct holiday.)

yule (*winter solstice*)—celebrated on or around december 21, this is the shortest day and the longest night of the year. witches will often decorate holiday trees, light yule logs, and share the joy of the sunlight's approaching return by giving and receiving gifts. the cold and darkness also give you the opportunity to look within, do some soul-searching, and tap into your resilience.

imbolg/imbolc—the midway point between yule and ostara is celebrated on or around february 1. the short, cold winter days are finally becoming a little longer and a little sunnier. spring is starting to feel like it's within reach. as the earth thaws, so will you, so make way for new happiness and new growth by doing a bit of spring cleaning—both literally and magically!

ostara (*spring equinox*)—this celebration of an equally long day and night is observed on or around march 21. sunlight continues to be more present throughout our days, which is something to celebrate—go on and have a nice outdoor lunch or host an ostara egg hunt. allow yourself to indulge in some chocolate bunnies while you're at it. nurture all the ways you've been growing.

bealtaine/beltane—the midway point between ostara and litha is usually celebrated on or around may 1. sunlight is now becoming plentiful, and the earth is finally awakening. hints of summertime are heavy in the air. this is often a day for love—handfasting (aka a pagan wedding ceremony) as well as coupling. consider donning a flower crown and having a bonfire, or do something else that speaks to your wild side.

litha (*summer solstice*)—usually celebrated on or around june 21, this is the longest day and the shortest night of the year—that means the sun is now shining in full force! celebrate the return of the light as well as all the things you have to be happy about. partake in summer activities like throwing a barbecue or swimming. wear a bathing suit with confidence.

lúnasa/lughnasadh—the midway point between litha and mabon is usually celebrated on or around august 1. summer is beginning to slip from your grasp, and you may begin to see some small signs of autumn. this is the first of the three harvest holidays, commonly observed by baking or eating bread and picking sunflowers. it's also a time to review your yearly growth.

mabon (*autumn equinox*)—our second celebration of equal day and night is usually observed on or around september 21. afterward, the nights will become longer and longer. in honor of the second harvest holiday, grab a pumpkin spice latte and go pick some apples and pumpkins. play in the vibrant leaves that are just beginning to fall. while you're at it, fall for *yourself*.

samhain—the midway point between mabon and yule is usually celebrated on or around october 31. autumn is departing; like it or not, winter is creeping in through the open door. the days are becoming very short, leaving little sunlight. as this is the final harvest holiday, this is a great time to honor the past year, as well as your past in general, including your deceased loved ones and ancestors.

MAGICAL JOURNAL PROMPT: *some christian and secular holidays were inspired by the wheel of the year holidays, many of which were adapted from very old pagan festivals. go down the list i gave you above. which ones sound like familiar mainstream holidays to you? if applicable, how can you integrate these wheel of the year holidays into some of your already-existing traditions?*

as the wheel of the year turns, you can add seasonal decorations to your altar (e.g., small holiday trees for yule or autumn leaf garlands for mabon), switching them out for the next holiday. think of it as another way to honor mother earth's magic.

i live my life as deeply

& as dramatically as

the earth lives her seasons—

i let myself feel

every little thing loudly,

& i don't care who's watching.

—go on, look upon me with equal awe & horror.

yule
soul-searching

if yule has the least sunlight of the entire year, then why is it such a merry day? why is it lovingly referred to as "witchmas"?

well, yule is essentially the darkest point before the dawn. after yule, sunlight will (very) slowly start returning to us—that's what we're ultimately celebrating, but that's not *all* we're celebrating. we're also celebrating the promise that our daily lives are about to change for the better.

soon, we'll get to stop being so cooped up in our houses to protect ourselves from the icy roads and frigid cold.

soon, we'll get to go back outside and connect with mother earth— bask in the glorious warmth and vitamin d we've missed so much.

soon, we'll get to feel a little more like ourselves again.

those are all fantastic things to look forward to; however, once the holiday trees come down, the yule logs get extinguished, and the gifts get put away, there will still be plenty of cold, dark days left.

it's still winter, after all.

depending on where you live, you'll have to deal with these things for at least a few more months, so why not go ahead and settle into the darkness? put on an oversized sweater. get yourself a cup of something warm and comforting (i'm fond of drinking orange clove tea in the winter— it's delish) so you can slow down and become better acquainted with one another.

the darkness is something to celebrate, too.

it's in our darkest hours—while everything is still and quiet—when we can finally turn within and explore our inner worlds, just like the seeds do in the ground before sprouting in the spring.

MAGICAL JOURNAL PROMPT: *time for some soul-searching. think back to a time when you felt lonely or isolated from others, whether it was by choice or not. what was the biggest thing this experience revealed about you?*

* * CARD SPREAD * *

CARD 1	CARD 2	CARD 3
who am i when i'm with others?	who am i when i'm by myself?	how can these two aspects of myself coexist?

yule
spell for resilience

perhaps you feel like you need a *little* more strength than usual to get through winter. while it's my second favorite season after autumn, even i can get restless near the end, when those cold days do nothing but drag and drag and drag. here's a spell you can cast around yule—or at any time during winter, really—to help you build your resilience. you're going to make it through this season just fine, lovely!

WHAT YOU'LL NEED
a gold candle in a holder
a small to medium tray
evergreen needles
a lighter or match

DIRECTIONS

place your gold candle in the middle of your tray.

sprinkle evergreen needles in a circle around the candle. (you can also use rosemary as a more practical option!)

as you light your gold candle, say the following affirmation: "i do make it through these remaining winter days. i am as resilient as an entire forest of evergreen trees. no amount of cold—or even an avalanche of snow—can topple me. so mote it be."

if you have the time, i recommend that you hang out and let your candle burn all the way down. as you do, imagine the flame and the evergreen (energetically) working together to help strengthen your resilience.

✳ ✳ CARD SPREAD ✳ ✳

CARD 1	*CARD 2*
what makes me resilient.	how i can tap into my resilience this season.

imbolg
emerging from your cocoon

by the time imbolg rolls around, the signs of winter are beginning to fade. the air should be starting to warm up and the snow should be starting to melt, getting ready for new growth. you may start to see signs of spring soon, like birdsong and small patches of flowers in your yard.

snowdrop flowers bursting through melting snow is my absolute favorite imbolg imagery.

maybe it's just the sensitive poet in me, but here's how i see it: when it's finally time for the snowdrops to be reborn, they take the name of the thing that prevented them from growing in the first place. they don't forget the lessons they learned from the frost while hiding deep within the cold soil; they let them become part of them, strengthen them.

hex, they even have the audacity to *look* like snow.

how metal.

when you finally emerge from your cardigan cocoon, remember what it was like to brave the cold. that version of yourself is what will help carry you into spring.

you're so close now.

while the earth is getting ready for new growth, get ready for *your* next evolution:

rummage through your hidden spaces—sometimes when i don't see
certain material things, i forget that they're there, which proves to me
that i didn't need them much in the first place. if this sounds like you,
go through your closets, drawers, and cabinets. donate anything in
good shape and trash anything too unsalvageable.

spruce up your social media—tidy up your posts as well as your following lists. get rid of anything that holds you back from growing into the person you most want to be.

do some home/space cleansing—use sound or smoke to energetically cleanse your altar as needed. this is also an excellent time to energetically cleanse your home.

MAGICAL JOURNAL PROMPT: *your habits—what you've been doing or thinking—may also need spring cleaning. what needs to be left behind with the winter version of you?*

* ✴ CARD SPREAD ✴ *

CARD 1	*CARD 2*
something to dust off and use.	something to pack away for a while.

imbolg
home cleansing

there are many ways to magically cleanse your space. personally, i prefer a cleansing simmer pot. not only is it effortless, but it smells incredible. as the steam rolls off the water, it energetically cleanses your entire home. below is a version i do on/around imbolg.

WHAT YOU'LL NEED
a small cooking pot
tap water
melted snow (optional)
a stovetop/burner
dried rosemary sprigs
dried lavender buds
a large cooking spoon

DIRECTIONS

fill your cooking pot halfway with tap water. if you have snow, add a handful to the pot. (you can wait until it snows, gather some, and save it in the freezer. otherwise, ice cubes work fine.) as the snow melts, winter's energy will also melt away from the nooks and crannies of your home.

let the water come to a boil on your stovetop or burner.

carefully add your rosemary sprigs (for cleansing) and lavender buds (for a dash of spring; many witches use it for cleansing as well) to the boiling water. continue to boil for a few more minutes. (i don't know if there are any rules to this, necessarily, but i basically boil it until i can start to smell the herbs strongly.)

stir the pot counterclockwise with the spoon and say: "i hereby cleanse this home of winter's cold, icy energy. may it leave space for spring's warmth and rejuvenation in its wake. so mote it be."

in magic, a *clockwise* motion manifests/creates; a *counterclockwise* motion releases/banishes.

turn the heat down and let the water come to a consistent simmer.

i usually let my simmer pots do their thing for anywhere from three to five hours. make sure you sit somewhere you can watch over it, especially if you have kids or pets. set a timer on your phone and come back every thirty to forty minutes to replenish any water that's evaporated. once you're finished, drain the pot and toss/compost the herbs.

* ✳ CARD PULL ✳ *

how might
i blossom
this spring?

151

everyday ways to cleanse your home

while imbolg is a great time to magically cleanse your home, it shouldn't be the *only* time you do it. you wouldn't clean your toilet only once a year, would you? (i mean, i sure hope not, but i won't judge!) personally, i try to do some kind of home cleansing every full moon—sometimes every other— since it's a good time to banish any negative energy that might be stuck in my space.

use sound or smoke—ring your bell or light your herb bundle/incense and then walk counterclockwise (starting at each door or threshold) through each room in your home, letting the sound/smoke cleanse all that bad stuff away. this is probably the most basic home cleansing method there is, so i think every witch should try it at *least* once.

sweep—witches can't actually fly on brooms, but one thing we *can* do is magically cleanse with them. for this, i recommend buying or making a special broom known as a *besom*. after you've swept with your regular broom, walk counterclockwise around your home, using your special broom to sweep the air—or the energy—just above the floor. open your door and sweep it out.

use fire and water—light a white candle and (carefully, very carefully!) walk from room to room, moving in counterclockwise circles. you can stop there, but if you'd like, you can also grab some full moon water and flick some around each room, being mindful of anything that can be damaged or ruined by water, such as books or electronics.

do a more everyday simmer pot—some of my favorite cleansing simmer pot ingredients are rosemary (which cleanses), lemon slices (which purify), and whole cloves (which protect against negative energy). you can follow the directions for the imbolg simmer pot, subbing out these ingredients for the ones used in those instructions.

MAGICAL JOURNAL PROMPT: *try at least three of these home cleansing methods. which one resonated the most with you? is there one you think you won't do again? why? personally, i think the sweeping method is great in theory, but i find it takes a little too much labor, so i mostly stick to the others.*

ostara
ditching the idea of "guilty pleasures"

i'll be honest: ostara isn't my favorite. when it comes down to it, it's basically the witch's easter, a holiday i celebrated as a child but never really enjoyed. ostara shares a lot of the same imagery and traditions, so it can be difficult for me to connect with.

but i do still try—for me—because there's plenty about this holiday that's valuable.

it's not just a day when i recognize that sunlight and moonlight have come back into perfect balance after months of darkness or all the greenery is making its long-awaited return.

it's also a day where i bring *myself* back into balance.

it's common to celebrate the themes of fertility, growth, and rebirth by eating sweets and baked goods. eating *is* a way of rebalancing yourself—as long as you don't guilt yourself over it. shaming yourself for "overdoing it" (whatever that means) or planning how you'll "eat better tomorrow" (food has no morality) is the opposite of harmony, actually.

which brings me to the topic of guilty pleasures. quite frankly, i think they're bullshit. the only reason you would ever have to feel guilty over enjoying something harmless is because you're afraid other people will think less of you or even make fun of you for it.

i'm not going to lie—*they might.*

but at least you'll be content reading your romance novels, listening to taylor swift, and eating as many chocolate eggs as you want. meanwhile, they'll be off in a corner being miserable because they can't stand watching others experience the joy they won't allow for themselves, all so they can feel a false sense of superiority.

which one sounds better to *you?*

MAGICAL JOURNAL PROMPT: *have you ever referred to something as your "guilty pleasure"? what is it and why does it make you feel guilty? now, reclaim it by writing: "i allow myself to revel in the things that bring me harmless happiness, including _____. so mote it be."*

✳ CARD SPREAD ✳

CARD 1	CARD 2	CARD 3
what am i denying myself right now?	why am i doing this?	how can i move past this restriction?

ostara

spell to nurture your growth

as the flowers have bloomed, so have you. but flowers don't just grow and stay vibrant forever. you have to keep nurturing them with things like sunlight and water throughout the season. some say kind words of encouragement help them prosper as well. the same goes for you. do this spell to nurture your own growth on ostara.

WHAT YOU'LL NEED

a small to medium basket

green ribbon

scrap paper

a writing utensil

3 fillable plastic eggs

a chocolate bunny

DIRECTIONS

place your small basket (or bowl) on your altar.

inside your basket, place your green ribbon (green yarn or easter grass— preferably the biodegradable kind—works, too) so it covers the bottom. this is meant to represent grass and mother earth's nurturing embrace.

tear your scrap paper into three medium pieces. on each one, write one positive way you've grown as a person since winter.

these will need to be things you'd like to keep nurturing so they can continue going strong. they can include small new habits like waking up a little earlier to pull your daily tarot card or something as life-changing as going sober from drugs or alcohol. (this isn't a replacement for treatment; it should serve as magical inspiration for you to seek real-world healing.)

slip each piece of paper into an egg of its own. as you do, repeat an encouraging affirmation, like, "i am fully capable of sustaining my new wakeup routine/sober lifestyle."

close your eggs and put them in your basket. as you add your chocolate bunny (or a chocolate bar, if need be) to the basket, say, "so mote it be." (chocolate is comforting; here, it symbolically nurtures your growth. feel free to eat it after you're done!)

* ⋇ CARD PULL ⋇ *

what steps
can i take to
sustain my new
spring growth?

bealtaine
do no harm but take no shit

in my poetry collection, *flower crowns & fearsome things*, i explore how complicated it is to be a human. we are never just one thing all of the time—some parts of us can be gentle and vulnerable, like wildflowers; other parts can be fierce and devastating, like wildfires.

around bealtaine, you'll notice that sunlight and greenery are continuing to grow in abundance and the summer heat is starting to cling to your skin. like many witches, you can celebrate by putting on a flower crown and dancing around a bonfire. dance to honor every aspect of yourself—your gentle as well as your fierce.

this seems like a good time to talk about the concept of "do no harm but take no shit" common among modern witches.

i actually *really* love this idea.

in my practice (and life), this looks like never intentionally doing harm to another person (my gentle side) while also never standing by and letting any harm come to me at the hands of another (my fierce side).

there are many ways to interpret the phrase "take no shit." for some witches, this means cursing/hexing those who have wronged them, aka practicing baneful magic. as you know by now, that isn't my style. (i won't shame you if it's yours; i just can't help you.)

here are some simple but still-effective methods you can use:

moving along—if a troll happens across your path, or if someone starts
   issues for the sake of it and can't be reasoned with, mute or block
   (literally or figuratively). just walk away. give your energy to something
   that matters instead.

standing up for yourself—is someone gossiping about you or trying to do irreparable harm to your character? okay, you can't just stand by and let that happen. call them out on their nonsense.

sending them love—counteracting people's bad behavior with kindness often takes them aback and makes them reevaluate what they are doing. (plus, the look on their face is usually *priceless*.)

MAGICAL JOURNAL PROMPT: *does the concept of "do no harm but take no shit" resonate with you? in what way?*

* * CARD SPREAD * *

CARD 1	*CARD 2*
me at my most vulnerable.	me at my most devastating.

bealtaine
spell jar to let loose your wild

one theme associated with bealtaine is your *wild*—who you are without the influence of people's passing judgments, bullying, or beauty industry sales tactics. these are things you might hide, dampen, or change because they're not accepted by society. connect with the authentic and down-to-earth version of yourself with the help of this spell jar.

WHAT YOU'LL NEED
"wild" things from nature (keep reading!)
a medium to large jar with a lid

DIRECTIONS

before your spell, go outside and collect some "wild" things—anything you like that you would happen across in nature, such as moss, flowers, clovers, tree bark, and rocks/pebbles.

just don't pick anything you can't identify (it could be dangerous), and don't go around picking flowers from other people's gardens or defacing trees for their bark (find fallen bark or even small twigs instead). be mindful and respectful.

when you get back to your altar to do your spell, layer your items inside of your jar however you would like. for each of the items you put in it, take a moment to envision something you want to do to let loose your wild.

perhaps you want to go braless, or perhaps you want to stop wearing gender-conforming clothing. perhaps you want to grow your body hair out or shave it all off. perhaps you want to go back to laughing loudly and freely after other people have criticized you for it for years. (can you tell this one was a *little* bit personal?)

once you're finished, put the lid on your jar.

hold the jar in your hands and repeat the words, "i am my wild and my wild is me. from this point forward, i vow to be nothing other than my pure, beautiful, and unrestrained self for all to see."

as you say "so mote it be," take the lid off of the jar to energetically symbolize letting loose your wild.

keep this jar on your altar for as long as you want, composting/tossing the ingredients when you're done.

* ✳ CARD PULL ✳ *

what does
complete and
wild freedom
look like for me?

litha

appreciating your sunny days

it's litha. it's finally hot enough for people to be walking around wearing tank tops, shorts, and their cutest pair of sandals. the sun is shining brightly up in the sky; in fact, this day contains more sunlight hours than any other day of the year. by the time you get ready for bed, the sun may only just be *starting* to set.

this is a long and cheerful day—one made for barbecues, backyard swimming, boardwalk adventures, water parks, and beach days.

no matter what you choose to do, take advantage of the light while it's here.

it won't be like this forever, you know.

after today is over, the sun will gradually set earlier and earlier, and the air will eventually become cooler and cooler.

of course, you still have *plenty* of time to enjoy nature and explore countless amazing summer experiences, but doesn't it seem like time passes the quickest when you're having the most fun? (maybe that's just me . . .)

what i love most about litha is how it teaches us a lesson that goes far beyond the season.

appreciate the sunny days in your life because you never know what could happen. tomorrow, the sky could open up and unleash an unexpected and devastating storm over you. while you're huddled in your shelter waiting for it to pass, you'll have all of those good times to hold on to.

they'll also remind you that you have plenty more to look forward to once it's all over.

the wheel of your life will *always* turn back in your favor again.

MAGICAL JOURNAL PROMPT: *what's your favorite summer memory—one that you can look back on to remind you that things can get better?*

* ✳ **CARD SPREAD** ✳ *

CARD 1	CARD 2
what makes me happy?	how can i spread that happiness to every part of my year?

litha
spell to reaffirm your beach body

this spell isn't about magically obtaining a beach-ready body—it's about accepting the fact that you already have one, because *every* body is a beach body. there's not a single thing you have to change about yourself before you put on your bathing suit and have some fun in the sun.

WHAT YOU'LL NEED
your fave bathing suit
a full-length mirror

DIRECTIONS

before you head down to your local beach or swimming pool, put on your bathing suit.

next, find a full-length mirror.

as you look at your reflection, i want you to pretend as though you're looking at your best friend, because that's exactly what you're going to treat yourself like.

and what do best friends do? hype each other up!

if you haven't already, go ahead and give yourself a warm and welcoming smile. look yourself in the eye as you shower yourself with compliments along the lines of, "omg, you look absolutely incredible!" and "that top looks super-cute on you, witch." (try to avoid using words such as *flattering*, which are often euphemisms for "makes you look skinny." you don't have to look thin to look good.)

now, talk back to your reflection and agree with them, and say "so mote it be."

although this may seem like an overly simple spell, i think choosing to unconditionally love and accept your body in a society that's constantly telling you what's wrong with it is *extremely* powerful magic.

* ✳ CARD PULL ✳ *

what can i
do to be nicer
to my body
today?

lúnasa
beginning your harvest

lúnasa is the first of three harvest holidays.

in my area, this is when people start harvesting—or picking—ripe peaches and nectarines. wheat is also harvested, which is then used to make bread, so witches refer to this as the "bread holiday" (which is adorable).

it's common to celebrate this harvesting of food; after all, it nurtures our bodies and gives us the energy we need to live our lives. that's certainly something we should all show appreciation for, witch or not.

i think it's also important to celebrate another type of harvest, too— your own personal harvest.

at this point, you're nearing the end of the year. it will be samhain before you know it. you've undoubtably done a lot so far, so make sure you take a moment to think about all the progress you've made toward your personal goals. harvest all of your wins and successes by taking special note of them. pat yourself on the back for a job well done—you deserve it!

at the same time, start thinking about the things in your life that have been positive forces but have grown as much as they possibly can. what needs to be harvested and enjoyed one last time—for now *or* for good—so you can continue to expand in new ways?

for example, i started my career by writing poetry collections, but then i cocreated an oracle deck, which put me on a totally new and different path. i'm at a point now where i'm soon going to be releasing my last poetry collection for the foreseeable future so i can work on witchcraft- related projects such as this.

i'm not saying goodbye to writing poetry (at least i don't think i am), but i'm putting it on pause, as it's not helping me expand in the ways i want to expand. maybe it can in the future. for now, i'm happy for the journey and all the successes i saw from it, but i'm ready for some new journeys. perhaps you are, too.

MAGICAL JOURNAL PROMPT: *what does your personal harvest look like this year?*

* * CARD SPREAD * *

CARD 1	CARD 2	CARD 3
something that still needs time to grow before harvesting.	something i can harvest rn.	something to harvest, enjoy, and let go of for good.

lúnasa

spell to treat yourself

you deserve to treat yourself after everything you've put effort into this year. this spell helps you celebrate that and acts as fertilizer for future endeavors. since this is the beginning of the harvest season—an undoubtably food-centric time—why not do a spell that incorporates some easy kitchen magic?

WHAT YOU'LL NEED
a butter knife
sunflower butter
a piece of bread
a plate
sunflowers and a vase with water (optional)

DIRECTIONS

use the butter knife to spread sunflower butter onto the bread. serve yourself with a nice plate. (it's a special occasion!)

if you have sunflowers, trim their stems and put them in a vase with water. place them wherever you're choosing to eat, whether it's at a table or at your altar. artificial sunflowers are fine, too.

why all the sunflowers, you ask?

sunflowers are harvested at this time, and they're also associated with happiness and good luck. you deserve both of those things and more, especially as you head into the remainder of the harvest season.

there's still plenty of time for you to do and harvest so many amazing things.

as you eat your bread, think ahead to everything you would like to harvest—
or accomplish—before the end of the season.

before you take the final bite of your bread, say, "i have already accomplished
so much this year and only continue to do so. i am now accomplishing all
of these things and more: (here's where you list them off!). so mote it be."
encouragement goes a long way!

clean up and display the sunflowers on your altar.

* * CARD PULL * *

an action i can
take to harvest
my immediate
dreams/goals
asap.

mabon
drinking pumpkin spice for protection

we continue the harvest season with our second harvest holiday, mabon.

the air is crisping up, making your nose adorably red. you look up to
see trees filled with brilliantly changing yellow, red, and orange leaves.
your social media feeds are packed with people wearing scarves and
picking pumpkins with their friends, families, and partners. you might
suddenly get inspired to bake an apple pie.

this is thought of as the witch's thanksgiving, so continue taking stock of your personal harvest and showing gratitude for yourself.

if you share this day with anyone else, make sure you express gratitude for them as well! you're amazing on your own, but there are surely those who bring value to your life, too, and they deserve to feel appreciated.

around this time, people start drinking pumpkin spice lattes. as i write this today, the #psl is officially back and everyone is just a *little* bit happier than they were yesterday—oh, the undeniable magic of pumpkin spice!

no, but really—did you know that pumpkin spice actually has a *ton* of magical properties? it's especially awesome for prosperity, confidence, and protection workings.

self-protection is vital, especially now, as you're harvesting some of your most impressive and long-awaited accomplishments. not everyone will look on with awe and pride; some will look on with envy and jealousy, and that bad energy—intentional or not—could cause you to stumble.

i once knew someone who said that they wished someone we both knew would get into an accident. a few days later, they did and were badly injured. i won't claim that person's bad energy caused the accident, but i'm sure it didn't help. (yes, they were extremely regretful!)

every time you drink your pumpkin spice latte, make sure you whisper an affirmation of protection into it first. just in case.

* ✳ CARD SPREAD ✳ *

CARD 1	CARD 2	CARD 3
who has made me feel supported this year?	what has made me feel safe?	a small way to enjoy the remaining autumn days.

everyday methods for self-protection

here are a few more ideas for protecting your energy, especially when it's not #psl season. you should eventually get to a place where you're implementing protection every day—not just before spellwork, but before you do *anything*! the same goes for cleansing and grounding. try a routine of cleansing, grounding, and protecting yourself upon waking up.

moisturize—after you do a shower cleanse, take your preferred lotion and dab it on your finger. using your lotion, create pentacle shapes on your skin, then rub it in like normal. this will create an invisible protective barrier for the day.

enchant your jewelry—take any piece of jewelry (e.g., a necklace, ring, or bracelet) and lay it in a dish filled with rosemary for at least a few hours. this will charge it with protective energy. when you're ready, put it on and find peace of mind knowing you're safe.

imagine it—close your eyes and picture a solid light in the color of your choice enveloping and protecting your body. easy af.

* ✳ CARD SPREAD ✳ *

CARD 1	CARD 2
the thing i need the most protection from at the moment.	the measures i can take to make sure i'm safe and sound.

mabon
spell to fall for yourself

as the leaves fall, why not do a spell to help *you* fall for yourself?

WHAT YOU'LL NEED
your magical journal

a writing utensil

scrap paper

3 autumn leaves

tape

a small to medium tray

acorns, chestnuts, or maple seeds (optional)

DIRECTIONS

MAGICAL JOURNAL PROMPT: *make a list of reasons you're worthy of falling for. avoid your physical attributes as much as possible; instead, describe your spirit. are you the kind of person who always lets people merge in front of them on the highway? are you a loyal friend? are you exceptionally trustworthy or helpful? go with things like that!*

when you're done with your list, pick three of your favorite reasons. tear up your scrap paper and write one reason on each piece.

next, you're going to tape your papers to your autumn leaves—one reason per leaf. they'll be flatter and easier to work with if you have pressed them between the pages of a large book for a few days beforehand.

if you don't have autumn leaves where you live, then any naturally fallen leaf will do. alternatively, you can buy artificial autumn leaves from the craft store or draw and color some autumn leaves and cut them out.

lay your leaves in the middle of your tray, pausing to say each reason aloud, using this format: "i am worth falling for because _____." after you say your last reason, say, "therefore, like these leaves, i choose to fall for myself each and every day. so mote it be."

if you want to add an extra touch of magic, you can surround your leaves with other signs of autumn like fallen acorns, chestnuts, or maple seeds (those fun helicopter things).

leave the tray on your altar for as long as you'd like; this past fall, i kept it set up for a few weeks because it was almost like fall altar decor and it made me happy to look at every day.

✳ ✳ CARD PULL ✳ ✳

how can i
keep loving
myself through
my changes?

samhain
honoring your past

samhain is the overwhelming favorite wheel of the year holiday among witches—and that includes me!

some witches even deem it so important that they refer to it as *the witch's new year.*

i can see why. it's the one day of the year when everyone's celebrating magic, as samhain is usually observed on or around halloween. (yes, our beloved halloween evolved from none other than samhain!)

this is also the only day of the year you can dress up as witchily as possible and no one will even give you strange looks for it. not that being a witch means you have to dress up any certain way—you don't—but it's much easier to wear a witch hat, for example, when so many nonwitches are walking around wearing them, too.

as it's yet another harvest holiday, it makes sense for you to continue thinking about all the things you've harvested this year. (doing this while eating handfuls and handfuls of halloween candy—aka your physical harvest—wouldn't be totally off-theme, either!)

since this is also the *last* harvest holiday, it means saying goodbye to this yearly cycle. as you do, make sure you also give a special thank-you to this year's version of yourself that will soon, too, be in the past—*forever*.

we move on so fast that we can forget entire periods of our lives. i look back sometimes and realize how many years are just . . . gone. i couldn't tell you a single thing that happened—not one memory, not one feeling, not one experience. it's like opening up a book and starting to read it from the middle.

what a shame it is to forget the people i've been before, the people who made my existence possible today—this is why it's so important that you journal, not just to keep track of your spellwork, but to keep track of who you are and where you've been. remember *all* of your magic, not just the intentionally witchy kind.

MAGICAL JOURNAL PROMPT: *who were you this year? interpret that question however you would like.*

* ＊ CARD SPREAD ＊ *

CARD 1	*CARD 2*	*CARD 3*
the most important lesson of my year.	the most important blessing of my year.	something from my year that deserves to be remembered.

samhain
spell to honor your dead

another way to honor your past is to honor your loved ones who are no longer on this earth. the veil between our world and the spirit world is said to be its thinnest on samhain; therefore, many witches choose to invite their deceased loved ones to a silent supper. let's start small by having a snack with them!

WHAT YOU'LL NEED
a black candle in a holder

a lighter or match

a snack (i recommend something with rosemary, as it represents remembrance)

photos or mementos of your loved ones

DIRECTIONS

before you begin, light your black candle to make sure your space is nice and protected from unwanted or negative energies. (this is important whenever you're doing spirit-related work, especially on a night like samhain, when so many are roaming about. i don't say this to scare you; i say this to make sure you do what you need to do to keep yourself safe!)

prepare your snack—a portion of which will be for your loved one(s)—and bring it over to your altar/table. out of respect, make sure you place their portion down first, as you would for a guest.

next, arrange their pictures or mementos by their place setting. make it clear who it's for by saying, "<u>name(s)</u>, i would love if you enjoyed a little snack with me."

as you eat, have a moment of silence for their lives. look at their photos/ mementos and reminisce. in your mind, catch them up on whatever they may have missed since they've been gone. tell them how much you love them and miss them. (i truly believe they're able to hear your thoughts, or at the very least feel the energy you're sending their way.)

when you're done, say, "thank you for coming. may your memory always be clear in my heart. so mote it be." blow out your candle. feel free to eat their snack once they've left—they won't mind!

* * CARD PULL * *

as the veil thins,
who—or what—
will be revealed
to me?

everyday ways to connect with your dead

i connect with my deceased loved ones and ancestors on a daily basis. i believe it helps my loved ones live on and stay part of my life. and by connecting with all those who came before me (aka my ancestors), i can learn from them and get a better idea of who i am and who i might come to be. in my experience, they want to use their energy to help me create magic, too.

some might be hesitant to connect with their ancestors either because they were toxic people or because they simply didn't know them. that's fine.

please know that you don't have to connect with anyone you don't want to. there are plenty of other connections for you to make as a witch, like with yourself or with mother earth. but you can also choose a lineage that you were not born into but feel close to, like an adoptive or found family. you'll also still be able to form a relationship with ancestors you have never met.

set up an altar—create a small space where you can go when you want to connect with them. place photos, heirlooms, or a dish of rosemary to create a focus for your altar. i find that keeping a candle there and lighting it before i talk/vent to them really sets the spiritual tone.

ask for a hand—if you're having trouble and need outside advice, go over to your altar. ask them a clear question then pull a tarot/oracle card to represent their answer. try to be as objective as possible when you interpret it. you can also ask them to join in on your spells if you want a magical boost or just some extra support while you do your thing.

do things they'd appreciate—for example, when i want to honor my late sister, i visit the beach, which she always loved to do. i truly believe she's there by my side enjoying it as much as i am. in my experience, they appreciate any effort, big or small. however, just living life on your own terms and making the best decisions for you is a way to honor their legacy. you're a part of them and vice versa, so they want nothing more than to see you happy and thriving.

✳ CARD SPREAD ✳

CARD 1	CARD 2	CARD 3
the best way to honor my dead (aka your deceased loved ones and/or ancestors).	the best way to honor myself.	the best way to do both at the same time.

mercury retrograde

when mercury is retrograde, it looks like it is moving backward, but it's not.

it's just an illusion—a trick of the eye.

mercury retrograde only happens a few times a year and lasts a few weeks, but a *lot* of people dread it and the backward energy it brings, especially when it comes to things like communications, technology, and travel.

your plane, train, or taxi could be delayed.

you could accidentally send a sensitive text to the wrong person.

your laptop could break at the worst possible moment.

you could have a huge misunderstanding with someone close to you.

you could have an ex show up out of the blue and cause you some confused feelings.

the inconveniences really add up and make it seem like everything that can possibly go wrong *is* going wrong, but that's not actually the case— that's only how it *appears* to you.

i'll be the first to admit that sometimes chaos happens with literally no rhyme or reason; however, in my opinion, the chaos that happens during mercury retrograde is usually the kind of chaos with *purpose*.

dig a little deeper, and you'll find that it always has something to teach you.

some people refuse to sign contracts during this time, but i've signed a few during mercury retrograde and it turned out fine. i just took extra steps to make sure everything was in order—i read them through a few times, asked all the important questions, and so on.

mercury retrograde gives you the opportunity to move more slowly and to think more carefully about things. it can also emphasize what isn't working too great so you can take some much-needed action.

my advice: stay grounded, do everything with careful thought, and prepare for the worst-case scenario. you'll survive.

MAGICAL JOURNAL PROMPT: *have you ever had a mercury retrograde moment? looking back, what advice would you give yourself to get through it?*

✵ ✵ CARD SPREAD ✵ ✵

CARD 1	CARD 2	CARD 3
what i can expect this mercury retrograde.	how to handle it with grace.	the valuable lesson it will teach me in the long run.

if you think she's stressed,
she's not.

it doesn't matter
what's thrown at them—

she'll find a way to deal.

—just let them grab their cauldron first.

feeling overwhelmed by the cycles

whew.

that was a lot for me to write, so i'm sure it was a lot for you to read.

by now, you might be feeling overwhelmed by how many cycles there are for you to potentially follow. (and i didn't cover anywhere near all of the potential cycles you can live by; this was just a sampling to get you started.)

i know. i've been there.

here are a few things for you to keep in mind moving forward:

you can incorporate them slowly—for example, when i began my practice, i only celebrated one or two of the wheel of the year holidays. as time went on, i slowly began to introduce more when i felt like i could handle them. i get how difficult this can be, especially if you're trying to keep up with all the other holidays, as well as all the other responsibilities in your life. this isn't a race, so please don't treat it like one!

you don't have to incorporate them at all—hey, opting out of the cycles entirely and doing magic whenever it feels right to you is okay in my book! maybe you want to observe some of the cycles and not others. or maybe you only want to work with certain parts of some cycles and skip the parts you don't vibe with. all of it is valid.

you don't have to observe them all the time—i used to release during every full moon and manifest during every new moon, but that got old really fast since i found that i didn't have things that needed to be released/manifested that often. now i partake only when i have specific things in mind. i also don't do a prosperity spell every single thursday, but when i do have a prosperity spell i want to work, i make sure it's *on* thursday—get it?

you don't have to go all out—you don't have to do a spell for every part of every cycle. giving it a silent acknowledgment can be enough—so can pulling a tarot card or eating a meal in honor of it. do whatever you have the energy for. doing magic when you don't feel like it probably won't be as effective, anyway.

just when she thought there was
no more magic to make,

they opened up their front door
& the twilight sky poured in

to remind her of her own
unending vastness.

—*larger than the whole damn universe.*

part iv

more magic

there's always more magic

we've almost reached the end of our time together, but luckily, there's still a little more magic to be made before we say our final goodbye and go our separate ways.

i thought it would be fun to include a few more spells for you to do. this section is intended to be a collection of workings that address things you may deal with in your everyday life—insecurities, self-acceptance, heartbreak. you may not need some of the spells right at this very moment, but there's a chance you will later!

with each working i've also written suggestions for specific cycles i think would make the most sense to align them with. they're merely suggestions, though, not requirements. as with all of the spells in this book, you can do them whenever you feel intuitively called to.

toward the end of the chapter, you'll find a spread that will come in handy when creating your own spells from scratch. if you'd like, you can jump headfirst into that part or come back to it whenever you feel ready. (if the very idea of it sounds terrifying to you, then that means it's probably time. do what scares you.)

MAGICAL JOURNAL PROMPT: *what's true at this point in your practice that wasn't true at the beginning of it? what do you think has been the biggest challenge so far? how has it served you and your life as a whole?*

spell to banish your insecurities

this is not a spell to banish—or release—the things you're insecure about. that wouldn't be very empowering, would it? instead, it's a spell intended to banish the feeling of insecurity itself. it won't get rid of your stretch marks, but it *will* (hopefully) get rid of the shame you feel whenever you look at them or think about wearing a crop top or shorts in public. (i highly suggest doing this spell in combination with the next one.)

BEST PERFORMED ON

saturday / full moon / samhain

WHAT YOU'LL NEED

your magical journal

a writing utensil

DIRECTIONS

MAGICAL JOURNAL PROMPT: *in your magical journal, write a list of your biggest insecurities. word each one like, "my insecurity about my _____."* *(this spell is designed for physical traits, but anything that comes to mind will work!)*

once you have your list, read it over.

afterward, repeat: "i've come to the conclusion that these insecurities no longer serve me. therefore, they're no longer welcome in my life. sorry (not sorry), but i just don't have time or energy for any of you anymore. you're hereby banished—*forever*. so mote it be."

take your writing utensil (preferably a pen or marker to represent permanence) and aggressively scribble out your list. keep going until you can no longer make out any of the words. rip into that paper. have absolutely no mercy as you banish your feelings of insecurity.

once you're satisfied, rip the page out of your magical journal. ball it up, stomp on it, ride your bike/car over it. throw it out somewhere far away from your house (without littering) so you can make sure you'll never feel any of those things ever again.

* * CARD SPREAD * *

CARD 1	CARD 2	CARD 3
my biggest insecurity.	what caused me to be insecure about it.	why it's a waste of my precious time and energy.

spell to accept your "flaws"

for this, you'll need to recall the physical traits you had feelings of insecurity about from the last spell. it's important to do more than just banish them and declare the job done. your flaws make you uniquely beautiful, so with this spell, you're going to bring in some love and acceptance.

BEST PERFORMED ON

friday / new moon / bealtaine

WHAT YOU'LL NEED
red/pink lipstick (optional—see directions)
sticky notes
a writing utensil
your magical journal

DIRECTIONS

apply the red/pink lipstick to your lips.

for each thing you were once insecure about, kiss one sticky note. (alternatively, if you're not comfortable wearing lipstick or just don't want to, you can kiss the sticky note without it on and it will still contain the same magical energy.)

place your sticky note in the corresponding place. for example, if you were insecure about the scars on your thigh, place one in that area. as you place each sticky note where it belongs, say, "this part of myself is deserving of love and acceptance, so love and acceptance is what i now give it."

when you place your last sticky note, say, "so mote it be."

187

when you're done, remove the sticky notes from yourself. label them with where they were placed, then stick them on a page in your magical journal. title the page "these parts of myself i have vowed to love and accept, no matter what."

MAGICAL JOURNAL PROMPT: *take it one step further. every once in a while, go back to the page with your sticky notes and pick one. do something to give that part of yourself extra love for the day—cherish it or showcase it in a special way and do so unapologetically. write about your experience after.*

* * CARD SPREAD * *

CARD 1	CARD 2
which of my unique flaws makes me the most beautiful?	how i can give it a metaphorical kiss.

do you think the ocean would ever
be embarrassed by the shape of her waves?

i will not be embarrassed by mine, either.

—*sacred curves.*

spell to mend your broken heart

chances are you'll have your heart broken one way or another—whether it's at the hands of a romantic partner, a friend, a family member, an idol, or maybe even yourself. sometimes your heart will break when a wish goes unfulfilled or when you've lost something important. no matter what your circumstance is, may this spell be a much-needed balm for your soul.

BEST PERFORMED ON
monday / waning moon / yule

WHAT YOU'LL NEED
red construction paper
scissors
a small to medium tray
dried peppermint leaves

DIRECTIONS

cut a heart shape out of your red construction paper, small enough to fit comfortably in your tray. (it helps if you fold the piece of paper in half, then draw a half-heart shape starting at the crease and moving up. cut your way along it, and bam, you have your heart!)

cut a zigzag line down the middle of your paper heart. place both pieces inside your tray, making sure the halves don't touch.

gaze upon the heart as you talk everything out. what happened? how does it make you feel? what are your worries and fears moving forward? cry if you feel called to. (this can be a healing process in and of itself.) get it all out.

take each half of the heart and piece them back together. say, "though this situation has caused me much pain, i recognize that it has taught me something valuable, even if i can't see it yet. i am choosing to mend it so i can put that lesson into action."

finally, sprinkle dried peppermint (if you don't have any, you can cut open a peppermint tea bag and use what's inside) over the now whole heart for an extra healing touch. when you're done, say, "so mote it be."

MAGICAL JOURNAL PROMPT: *if your best friend came to you with a broken heart, what advice would you give them? in your notes app or your magical journal, write them a draft of a text (don't send it!), then read it back to yourself. there's probably something in there that you need to hear, too.*

✶ ✳ CARD SPREAD ✳ ✶

CARD 1	CARD 2	CARD 3
who i was before the heartbreak.	who i'll be after.	the vital wisdom i've gained.

spell to stop doomscrolling

i don't know about you, but when something bad is happening in the world, i tend to go on social media and scroll through the various feeds for hours and hours, taking in all of the reactions. most of the time, i don't even mean to do it—it almost becomes hypnotic and it's impossible to stop. after a while, it gives me a screen headache and puts me in a horrible state of mind. if you experience this, too, then do this to nip it in the bud.

BEST PERFORMED ON
wednesday / waning moon / ostara

WHAT YOU'LL NEED
your phone
a small drawstring pouch or box
an amethyst crystal

DIRECTIONS

as soon as you show signs of doomscrolling (or any kind of hypnotic phone-scrolling, really), turn off your phone immediately. if you want to go the extra mile, then you can cleanse your phone using a bell as soon as it powers down.

put your phone into either a drawstring pouch or box and place it on your altar. put your amethyst crystal on top—along with all of its other amazing magical properties, it's also used to soothe addictive behaviors.

say, "my desire to doomscroll is gone. i do not distract myself from feeling my feelings, but i do not obsess over them, either. i am going to take the information i have learned—no matter how upsetting—and sit alone with it. from this point forward, i integrate screen time in a more beneficial way. so mote it be."

leave your phone there for as long as you're able to. i suggest at least three to five hours, if possible, or even the remainder of the day.

afterward, continue to keep informed of world events and raise awareness on social media. however, if it gets to the point of unhealthy fixation, take a break and come back when you feel better.

MAGICAL JOURNAL PROMPT: *what kind of relationship do you have with your phone? how does it impact your daily life? what about your witchcraft practice?*

⁎ ⁎ CARD PULL ⁎ ⁎

what peace
might i find if i
spend less time
on my phone?

tea spell to calm tf down

sometimes i just cannot get a handle on my nerves, so i drink this tea to help me calm tf down. i find i sleep better if i drink it an hour or so before bedtime, too. of course, this isn't a replacement for medical treatment (nothing in this book is), so seek that for any ongoing issues related to anxiety or insomnia!

BEST PERFORMED ON
monday / waning moon / yule / mercury retrograde

WHAT YOU'LL NEED
lavender and chamomile tea in a cup
honey or honey alternative
a spoon

DIRECTIONS

prepare your lavender and chamomile tea as directed.

make sure your space is calm and quiet before you begin—this is true before any spell, but it's especially so for this one.

if you'd like, you can wear something that's soothing to you, like a sweater or a blanket. you may choose to sit on a soft floor pillow or to hug a cherished stuffed animal friend—whatever helps, right?

add your honey or honey alternative (e.g., agave or maple syrup) into your tea. as you stir it all together (try to stir in a clockwise motion, as this spell is seeking to *create* calmness), say, "i am calm af. i am serene af. from this point forward, i have complete and total peace of mind. so mote it be."

sip on your tea in silence. acknowledge and release any uneasy thoughts that come up.

MAGICAL JOURNAL PROMPT: *what's something that gives you a magical sense of comfort?*

* ✳ CARD SPREAD ✳ *

CARD 1	*CARD 2*	*CARD 3*
the reason i'm freaking out.	why it isn't as big of a deal as i think.	a calm and practical solution.

the way she sees it,

she can either worry about
things she can't possibly control

or she can drink some tea,
maybe take a nap,

& then focus on what she *can* control.

—she highly recommends it, too.

spell to focus on what matters

do you ever have a task or something you know you need to do—answer
emails, clean the bathroom—but your mind is on just about everything
but that? do this spell to persuade it to focus on what matters. (it's also
perfect for things like test-taking or giving a presentation at work.)

BEST PERFORMED ON
wednesday / waxing moon / imbolg

WHAT YOU'LL NEED
a small to medium tray
the knight of swords tarot card
5–6 small rainbow fluorite crystals

DIRECTIONS

in the middle of your tray, lay down your knight of swords tarot card. (this knight in particular has a reputation for setting their sights on an idea and charging toward it—the exact energy you want as a result of this spell!)

arrange your rainbow fluorite crystals in a circle surrounding your knight.

sit and concentrate on the contents of the tray for a few moments—give your spell as much *focused* energy as you possibly can. do this for, say, three to five minutes. (think of it like a meditation with a specific magical purpose.)

next, say this affirmation: "all of my attention is focused on (task at hand) for (time frame). i get done what i need to get done in the timeliest and most efficient manner. as i do so, i am ever-calm, never stressed. the results are quality, not just quantity. so mote it be."

you might want to pluck one of the crystals from the tray and keep it on your person as you go about your task!

MAGICAL JOURNAL PROMPT: *which part of your magical practice could use a little more of your attention? have you been slacking on your tarot routine or putting off a spell you should have done weeks ago? maybe you have a witchy TBR you need to make a dent in?*

* ✳ CARD SPREAD ✳ *

CARD 1	CARD 2	CARD 3
the thing i need to get done.	the thing distracting me from it.	how to clear it so i can focus.

spell to own your amazingness

confession: i still get imposter syndrome about being an author. i've been on bestseller lists, i've won awards, i've had sold-out readings . . . yet i still go through periods when i doubt my abilities and convince myself that i'm a fraud who doesn't deserve any of this. if you ever go through similar moments of self-doubt, do this spell to own your amazingness!

BEST PERFORMED ON

tuesday / full moon / bealtaine

WHAT YOU'LL NEED

your magical journal

a writing utensil

a piece of scrap paper

a locket necklace

DIRECTIONS

MAGICAL JOURNAL PROMPT: *describe yourself like you're the badass main character in an epic fantasy novel. what are you known for? what are your accomplishments? don't be afraid to mix fact with fiction or brag a little.*

take a small piece of scrap paper and write down your favorite line from this description—the one that makes you feel unstoppable, the one that makes you feel good about being *you.*

roll—or fold—your scrap paper into a scroll as tiny as you need it to be, and then tuck it into the locket and close it back up.

hold the necklace in your hands as you say, "i am no imposter. i am exactly what i say i am: (the line from your self-description). no one and nothing can ever take that away from me, not even myself. so mote it be."

now you have a necklace that acts as a forever reminder that you're amazing!

* ✳ CARD PULL ✳ *

something to
remember when
i lose sight of how
amazing i am.

spell for self-forgiveness

the fact is that we're all humans and we're all capable of making mistakes; however, sometimes it can be difficult to cope with this. a better use of your energy would be to accept what you've done and learn to live with it. (note: this is *not* an alternative to taking accountability.)

BEST PERFORMED ON
friday / waning moon / imbolg

WHAT YOU'LL NEED
your magical journal
a writing utensil
an envelope
lavender sprigs
tape

DIRECTIONS

MAGICAL JOURNAL PROMPT: *i want you to write a letter forgiving yourself for your mistake—not excusing, forgiving. there is a huge difference. in your letter, make sure you include some plans to rectify your mistake (if needed/ possible) and do better moving forward.*

once you're done, read this letter aloud to yourself. fold the paper up and put it in your envelope. address the envelope to yourself (you can put your full address or just write your name on the front) and seal it.

after, take your lavender sprigs and tape them to the front of the envelope. (i find that lavender has a very gentle and forgiving energy.)

hold the letter in your hands and say: "self-compassion is beautiful, and i hereby give it to myself freely and without restraint. no longer do i punish myself for chapters long closed, for chapters that cannot be rewritten. self, know that i forgive you your missteps; even if you can't make this situation right, know that you still have time to make better decisions. so mote it be."

* ✳ CARD SPREAD ✳ *

CARD 1

a card to represent my mistake, plain as day, so i can face it.

CARD 2

why i should forgive myself.

CARD 3

how that self-forgiveness looks in action.

spell to be a lucky bitch

we all need an extra pinch of luck sometimes. this is a spell i would do if i were, say, trying to increase my odds when buying a car, making an offer on a house, applying to adopt a new cat, or otherwise hoping things go my way (for the good of all and with harm to none, as always). hope this can help you, too!

BEST PERFORMED ON
thursday / new moon / any harvest holiday

WHAT YOU'LL NEED
a green candle in a holder
a symbol of what you need luck for
a lucky personal item (optional)
a lighter or match

DIRECTIONS

put your green candle in the middle of your spellwork space.

to one side of the candle, place a symbol of what you need luck for, like a copy of a completed application. (if you don't have anything, write down a description of what you want.)

to the other side of the candle, place your lucky personal item. perhaps you have a lucky crystal, a lucky scrunchie, or even the cliché lucky pair of underwear. i won't judge no matter what it is.

light your candle. close your eyes. imagine in detail what it would be like to have this situation go in your favor. make sure you bring that feeling in when you say, "i am so overjoyed now that i have _____. i truly am one lucky bitch. may a lucky bitch i forever be." say this three times total, tying it up with "so mote it be."

let your candle burn down, if possible. wait and see what happens.

MAGICAL JOURNAL PROMPT: *in my opinion, any item you assign as lucky thus becomes magically lucky. what's your magically lucky item? what kind of luck has it granted you?*

* ✶ CARD SPREAD ✶ *

CARD 1	CARD 2
the current state of my luck.	how to stay in or get into the mindset of being the lucky bitch i am.

simmer pot spell to be a happy witch

do you ever just feel like you need a little positivity boost? do this simmer pot to coax out the happy witch within. (this is definitely *not* intended to treat or cure serious emotional issues. this spell is meant for lighthearted occasions only.) added bonus: some happy energy for your home, too!

BEST PERFORMED ON
sunday / a full or new moon / litha

WHAT YOU'LL NEED
a cooking pot
tap water
a stovetop/burner
orange slices
3 cinnamon sticks
a handful of whole cloves
a large cooking spoon

DIRECTIONS

fill your cooking pot halfway with tap water. let it come to a boil on your stovetop or burner.

as it's boiling, carefully add your orange slices (for happiness and joy), cinnamon sticks (for warmth and energy), and cloves (for protection against negative energy). let the water boil with everything in it for a few more minutes.

stir the pot clockwise as you say: "i am a happy witch. this is my happy home. no negative energy may here roam. so mote it be."

turn the heat down and let the water come to a consistent simmer.

let your simmer pot do its thing for anywhere from three to five hours. come back every thirty to forty minutes to replenish any water that's evaporated. once you're finished, go ahead and drain your pot. toss or compost the ingredients.

MAGICAL JOURNAL PROMPT: *write about something you can do to make your home or magical space a more pleasant place to be.*

* * CARD PULL * *

what's one
reason i should
be a happy witch
right now?

there are so many reasons
to be miserable
in a world such as this.

i mean, look around—
then try to see with new eyes,
even if for just a moment.

name at least one thing that,
despite it all, makes you
want to take another breath.

i'll go first:
you.

—inhale.

coffee spell for anything you want

didn't i tell you i would teach you how to do coffee spells? coffee spells
are extremely versatile and can be used for anything you want (like the
title suggests), as the caffeine in coffee energizes any intention you give it.
they're especially good for things you want to happen quickly—like, *right
now.* consider this a step toward creating your own spells.

BEST PERFORMED ON

any given morning

WHAT YOU'LL NEED

a cup of coffee

your normal coffee fixings

a spoon or stirrer

powdered cinnamon (optional)

DIRECTIONS

the first step is as simple as it gets: make a cup of coffee. put whatever creamer or sweetener in it that you like. (this spell also works with your favorite coffee-to-go.)

it's not required, but you can assign magical properties to your ingredients, too. for example, when i make my coffee in the morning, i add creamer with the intention of lightening my stress. when i add sugar, i do so with the intention of making my day a little sweeter. you can google common magical properties of your ingredients as well, but i'm not really that fancy with it on the everyday. i prefer short and simple personal correspondences.

as you stir your coffee (clockwise to manifest, counterclockwise to banish), say your affirmation. it can be something like, "i make it through this day stronger than ever before" (manifesting) or "i am amazing at dissolving all the challenges that come my way today" (banishing). personalize it for *your* day.

if you have powdered cinnamon, add a few shakes on top as you say, "so mote it be." because of cinnamon's fiery energy, it will energize your intention even further.

✶ CARD SPREAD ✶

CARD 1	*CARD 2*
what do i want to achieve the most right now?	how can i energize myself to go after it?

creating your own spell

alright, the time has finally come for you to create your own spell! refer to the magical journal prompts below when you have a topic in mind. you have no reason to be nervous. you've learned so much through reading and doing—all that's left is to implement it!

◆ why are you doing this spell? what is it that you hope to achieve by casting it?

◆ do you want to *manifest* or *banish* something? (if you're not trying to make something go away—or banish it—then you're probably trying to create something, aka manifest it.)

◆ when are you going to do your spell? using a combination of your witchy knowledge and intuition, decide based on what makes the most sense. (a certain day of the week? a moon phase? a wheel of the year holiday?)

◆ which tools will you use? this can mean crystals, herbs, candles, cards, or other magical-to-you objects. even if you're intuitively drawn to something, put into words why you've chosen them. don't include things just to include them; sometimes simpler *is* better.

◆ prewrite an affirmation to include in your spell. don't be thoughtless with this; really spend some time on this part because it's what everything else in your spell will revolve around. empower and encourage yourself with your words, and don't forget to word your intention as though it's already happened.

◆ which action will you take along with your words? you can do any combination of things, such as making a list, lighting a candle, or crafting a spell jar. if applicable, you might want to move in a clockwise circle to manifest or a counterclockwise circle to banish.

◆ once your spell is finished, draw an illustration of what it looked like. (or a few, depending on how many steps there were.) you don't need to be an artist to do this—this is just to help you if you ever plan to repeat the spell in the future.

◆ how did it go? self-reflect on how you feel about your spell immediately after, a week after, a month after, and even a year after. what were the short-term results? what about the long-term results? is there anything you'd like to do differently next time?

MAGICAL JOURNAL PROMPT: *do you have any fears or hesitations when it comes to creating your own spells? what can you do to overcome them, not just magically, but on a personal level? remember: the more you do it, the more comfortable you'll become.*

so this is goodbye?

though this particular book is now coming to an end, i beg you not to let it be the end of your magical journey.

let it be merely the beginning.

as you move forward on your path, you're almost certainly going to experience periods when you feel unmotivated to do spellwork or even forget that you have magic altogether. this happens to the most experienced witches, even the lifelong ones.

yes, even to me.

when—*not if*—it happens to you, don't fret too much, for your magic will always be there when you're ready to find it again. instead, use that energy to embrace your magical lulls. see them for what they are: an opportunity to rest before your next powerful chapter.

keep this book close. the second you begin to feel lost, crack it open again and go back to page 1. immerse yourself in these words. seek bits of inspiration wherever you can. remember your own unique inner moondust and perform one of my simple spells, or better yet, use them to inspire one of your own creation.

you can do this every year, if you'd like. start a few weeks before yule and slowly make your way back through all four parts. see the first spell as a rededication ritual of sorts where you remember—or add onto—your ethics as well as your magic.

~~goodbye.~~

see you some other time, whether it's within these pages or in brand-new ones.

laced with love,
amanda

MAGICAL JOURNAL PROMPT: *as we say so long for now, it's also time for you to say goodbye to the person you were before you decided to be a witch—all of the old beliefs that no longer serve you, all of those old self-limitations. get out your magical journal and write a heartfelt letter thanking past-you for everything that led up to that moment, and the way this decision has (hopefully) improved your mindset and life.*

references

Jessica Defino. "It's Time to Rethink the 'Trend' of Burning Sage on Instagram." *Fashionista*. https://fashionista.com/2019/11/burning-sage -cultural-appropriation.

special acknowledgments

◆ *my poet-spouse, parker lee*—thank you for listening to my dreams & for giving me the space as well as the support i needed as i slowly brought them to life. the spearmint lattes were a huge help, too. <3

◆ *my literary agent, lauren spieller*—thank you for believing i could write a book like this & be successful at it. without you & your tireless work, it wouldn't have found the amazing home it did. you're the BEST!

◆ *my RP team*—thank you not just for agreeing to publish this but for your incredible enthusiasm surrounding my work. it couldn't possibly be in better hands.

◆ *my beta readers*—thank you christine day, summer webb & mira kennedy for following me through the genre shift & for the honest feedback that helped this book become the best possible book it could be.

◆ *my friends & family*—thank you to those who are forever cheering me on, regardless of what i decide to write.

◆ *my readers*—thank you, thank you, thank you!!! just the fact that you would take a chance on my words means all the stars in the sky to me. i hope this book made you believe in your ability to make all of your dreams come true; if not, then i hope it will at least look really pretty on your bookshelf.

◆ *my illustrator, raquel aparicio*—thank you for the most magical illustrations a witchy writer could ask for!

about the author

amanda lovelace (she/they) is the author of several bestselling poetry titles, including her celebrated women are some kind of magic series as well as her you are your own fairy tale trilogy. they are also the cocreator of the *believe in your own magic* oracle deck & the *cozy witch* tarot deck & they are now the author of their very first witchcraft book, *make your own magic*. when she isn't reading, writing, or drinking a much-needed cup of coffee, you can find her casting spells from her home in a (very) small town on the jersey shore, where she resides with her poet-spouse & their three cats.

follow amanda

@ladybookmad

@ladybookmad

amandalovelace.com